Theology Brewed in an African Pot

Theology Brewed
in an
African Pot

Agbonkhianmeghe E. Orobator

ORBIS BOOKS
Maryknoll, New York 10545

Founded in 1970, Orbis Books endeavors to publish works that enlighten the mind, nourish the spirit, and challenge the conscience. The publishing arm of the Maryknoll Fathers and Brothers, Orbis seeks to explore the global dimensions of the Christian faith and mission, to invite dialogue with diverse cultures and religious traditions, and to serve the cause of reconciliation and peace. The books published reflect the views of their authors and do not represent the official position of the Maryknoll Society. To learn more about Maryknoll and Orbis Books, please visit our website at www.maryknoll.org.

Library of Congress Cataloging-in-Publication Data

Orobator, A. E. (Agbonkhianmeghe E.)
    Theology brewed in an African pot / Agbonkhianmeghe E. Orobator.
      p. cm.
    ISBN-13: 978-1-57075-795-2 (pbk.)
    1. Theology—Africa. 2. Theology, Doctrinal—Africa. 3. Achebe, Chinua. Things fall apart. I. Title.
BT30.A35O76   2008
230.096—dc22
                                            2008006043

To Mrs. Roseline Orobator
and
Mrs. Gloria Arabome

Two African mothers and theologians
who live by faith, love, and hope

Contents

Preface

In the beginning I had no intention to write this book. It all started in 1998, soon after I obtained a master's degree (also known as a licenciate) in theology from the Jesuit School of Theology at Berkeley, California. My Jesuit superior assigned me to work at the Jesuit novitiate in Benin City, Nigeria, even though I had no previous experience teaching theology. My class consisted of a small group of impressionable novices, eager to begin their formation in religious life. Over two years I developed an introductory course in theology, inviting them to reflect on the contents of their faith as Africans.

Seven years later I was invited to give a workshop to another group of Jesuit novices in Arusha, Tanzania. By that time I had my doctorate in theology and religious studies from the University of Leeds in England, and I was just beginning my teaching career at Hekima College Jesuit School of Theology in Nairobi, Kenya. This second invitation to introduce beginners to theology appeared providential. So I retrieved my notes from my earlier teaching stint in Benin and put together a small book to serve as an introduction to theology and also an account of my own faith as an African. This is the genesis and purpose of *Theology Brewed in an African Pot*.

Theology in Africa remains confined largely to a group of people I call "professional Christians," mostly men—there are a few women too—who make a living as ministers of the church: priests, religious, sisters, and brothers. Seminaries and institutions of religious formation serve as the privileged setting for doing theology. These people might find this book interesting and useful. The target audience belongs to a different category altogether, however, that of "non-professional Christians," men and women who simply live their faith. They might be amateur theologians, but this does not mean they are incapable of reflecting more deeply on the content of their faith and its implications for Christian living. *Theology Brewed in an African Pot* introduces theology to them and invites them to do theology. It also aims to inform readers from outside the continent who are interested in learning more about how theology is done in Africa.

I anticipate that a wide variety of readers will find this book useful—students of theology, lay Christians, religious and clergy in formation, and religious educators in Africa and on other continents. My primary concern is to write a book that is accessible to people who have a minimal or no background at all in academic theology. In this sense, the book integrates a catechetical element: it explores the content of faith, the primary themes of belief, and their implications for Christian living. It can also serve as a short course and a study guide. Each chapter ends with a set of questions for reflection and group discussion. To facilitate this encounter with theology, I have avoided footnotes and too many bibliographical references. For those who might become interested in delving deeper into theology in an African context, a short list of useful books is given at the end.

I have written this book as an *African Christian*. Each of these words carries significant implications for how I understand and live my faith. Another circumstance that influences my perspective relates to my religious history. I converted to Christianity at the age of sixteen. While the circumstances of my conversion were quite ordinary, I made a conscious decision to embrace and explore something new. Until my baptism as a Catholic, I lived the early part of my life within the milieu of African religion, being familiar with the gods, goddesses, divinities, deities, and ancestors of my people. I participated in many worship rituals in my family and developed a strong awareness of the communion between the human and the divine in daily life. As an African, prayer, praise, worship, and celebration were part of my upbringing.

Since converting to Christianity I have rediscovered the richness of my African religious heritage in surprisingly new ways as I live and pray as an African Christian. Many years after my conversion, both my African religious heritage and Christian faith come together in a way that I find meaningful, enriching, and deeply satisfying. Contrary to what some writers believe about African Christians, I do not feel torn between two worlds: I have a strong identity as an African Christian. I am at home as an African Christian. This book is thus also an invitation to explore the compatibility between Christian faith and African cultures.

My identity as an African Christian makes it impossible for me to separate talking about God from the practice of my faith. In Africa theology links naturally with spirituality, praise, worship, and prayer. My prayer as an African derives from my experience of God in the various circumstances of life.

Doing theology is not an isolated enterprise, particularly in Africa where doing theology is a community event. At Hekima College where I teach, one of my favorite classes is called simply "Palaver Session." This is the time when students sit in a round hut and talk about God, faith, and their religious experience in an African context. Sometimes we have something to drink and munch on as we dialogue, debate, and converse. As I will show in chapter 1, two characters from Chinua Achebe's well-known novel *Things Fall Apart*, Chief Akunna and Mr. Brown, seem to have done theology in a similar manner.

I owe a debt of gratitude to many people who have contributed to the writing of *Theology Brewed in an African Pot*. I am grateful to the novices of the Jesuit novitiate in Benin City and in Arusha who gave an attentive ear to my first attempts to articulate the contents of this book. My present students at Hekima College will recognize some of the materials from our introductory theology class. I have drawn on our animated conversations and their responses to questions to revise and rewrite some sections of it.

Finding the time and space to write this book proved to be a daunting task. Thanks to the generosity of T. Frank Kennedy, S.J., who invited me to the Jesuit Institute at Boston College as a visiting scholar, and my Jesuit colleagues T. Howland Sanks, William O'Neill, Tony Sholander, Kevin Burke, and Joe Doust, who invited me to the Jesuit School of Theology at Berkeley as adjunct faculty,

I found a conducive environment to complete the first draft of this book. Along with Jesuits David Hollenbach and Evaristus Ekwueme, they offered me the space, resources, and support that I needed to complete it. To them, a hearty "Thank you!" Bill O'Neill kindly read a draft of this book and offered useful comments. For their inspiration, support, and friendship, I thank Laurenti Magesa, Joseph Healey, M.M., Tony Azzarto, S.J., and Kpanie Addy, S.J. I am grateful to editor Susan Perry at Orbis Books for her interest and assistance with the publication of this book.

I owe a special debt of gratitude to all the members of my Jesuit Community at Hekima College for their unwavering support, encouragement, and companionship. *Asanteni sana!* My thanks also go to my friends at St. Paschal Baylon in Oakland, Christ the King in San Diego, and St. Joseph in Benin City.

I have reserved my deepest and fondest word of gratitude for Oghomwen n'Oghomwen Sr. Anne Arabome, S.S.S., and Fr. Chuks Afiawari, S.J. Your unfailing love and unshakeable belief in me make all things possible.

Nairobi, 2007

⟡

A Prayer for a Traveler

May the falling Iroko tree never block your path,
May the lightning bolt never strike near you,
May the roaring thunder ward off evil from your path,
May the vulture and birds of prey never trail you,
May the tree stumps and bush creepers never cause
    you to stumble.

May your presence bring blessing to all who show you
    hospitality,
May forest trees shade you from the sun's blazing
    anger,

May gentle streams of water refresh you when you are
    thirsty,

May wild fruits nourish you when you feel the pangs
    of hunger,

When night falls, may fireflies light up your path and
    chirping crickets keep you company.

Amen!

1

Chukwuka: Talking about God

Chinua Achebe's masterpiece, *Things Fall Apart*, is arguably the most famous literary account of the encounter between missionary Christianity and African traditional religious beliefs and practices. The setting for his story is a small but vibrant and dynamic village called Umuofia, somewhere in the eastern part of present-day Nigeria.

The small band of pioneer Christian missionaries who came to the village of Umuofia was led by a white man, Mr. Brown, who earned the respect of the people by his restrained and sensible approach to the deep religious differences that divided members of his church and the people of Umuofia. Chinua Achebe eloquently tells the story of an encounter between Mr. Brown and one of the leading men of the village, Chief Akunna.

> Whenever Mr. Brown went to that village he spent long hours with Akunna in his *obi* (hut) talking through an interpreter about religion. Neither of them succeeded in converting the other but they learned more about their different beliefs.
>
> "You say that there is one supreme God who made heaven and earth," said Akunna on one of Mr. Brown's visits. "We also believe in Him and call Him Chukwu. He made all the world and the other gods."
>
> "There are no other gods," said Mr. Brown. "Chukwu is the only God and all others are false. You carve a piece of wood—like that one" (he pointed at the rafters from which Akunna's carved *Ikenga* [ancestral staff] hung), "and you call it a god. But it is still a piece of wood."

1

"Yes," said Akunna. "It is indeed a piece of wood. The tree from which it came was made by Chukwu, as indeed all minor gods were. But He made them for His messengers so that we could approach Him through them. . . .

"Your queen sends her messenger, the District Commissioner. He finds that he cannot do the work alone and so he appoints *kotma* to help him. It is the same with God, or Chukwu. He appoints the smaller gods to help Him because His work is too great for one person."

"You should not think of Him as a person," said Mr. Brown. "It is because you do so that you imagine He must need helpers. And the worst thing about it is that you give all the worship to the false gods you have created."

"That is not so. We make sacrifices to the little gods, but when they fail and there is no one else to turn to we go to Chukwu. It is right to do so. We approach a great man through his servants. But when his servants fail to help us, then we go to the last source of hope. We appear to pay greater attention to the little gods but that is not so. We worry them more because we are afraid to worry their Master. Our fathers knew that Chukwu was the Overlord and that is why many of them gave their children the name Chukwuka—'Chukwu is Supreme.'"

"You said one interesting thing," said Mr. Brown. "You are afraid of Chukwu. In my religion Chukwu is a loving Father and need not be feared by those who do His will."

"But we must fear Him when we are not doing His will," said Akunna. "And who is to tell His will? It is too great to be known."

Let us begin at the beginning: What is this subject called theology? The definition of any subject allows us to demarcate its boundary, understand its nature, and grasp its object. If we begin with the word itself, we get an idea of what theology is about. "Theology" is a composite of *theos* and *logos*. Both words come from the Greek language: *theos* means God and *logos* means word. Put together they mean our word on God and about God. We can define theology simply as our study of God—how and what we know about God. Whether or not it is possible to know God or know something about God is another question, but it is safe to assume that when we say or hear the word *God*, we at once form an idea of what it means and know a thing or two about the reality the word represents for us. This is the core of the domain or discipline called theology. It is that simple.

We need to dispel the notion that theology is the exclusive preserve of experts and academicians. Theology is something that we all *do* all the time, even without actually paying attention to it. I find no better illustration of this than the conversation given above between Mr. Brown and Chief Akunna. The former had probably spent a few years studying the Bible and theology in his native England to prepare for his missionary journey to the African village of Umuofia. He possessed an impressive mastery of the religious vocabulary and could reel off the theological terminologies with ease. Chief Akunna had not received any formal theological training in the knowledge of his religion. Notwithstanding, he possessed a native sense of religion that made him a theologian of no lesser stature and repute than Mr. Brown. He knew how to talk sensibly about God—the nature of God, the meaning of worship, mediation and creation, divine providence, and divine retribution.

In the course of this engaging conversation between Mr. Brown and Chief Akunna we get a clear idea of the meaning of theology: *talking sensibly about God.*

Three Stories and Some Questions

In order to open up the meaning of theology in simple terms I turn to three stories from the Gospels. Most Christians will be familiar with these stories. Each story presents an aspect of the meaning of theology and together they will help us create a fuller picture of its object, nature, and method. The first story is from the Gospel according to the tradition of John.

In John 3:1-21 we read the interesting story of an encounter between Jesus and a man named Nicodemus. This man comes to see Jesus under the cover of darkness. He is interested in resolving some of the burning questions concerning his faith. He desires to know how it is possible for someone to be "born again" in order to enter the kingdom of God. Perhaps much to Nicodemus's disappointment, Jesus does not give a direct answer to his questions. In response Jesus veers off on an elaborate monologue on the flesh and the spirit, earthly and heavenly things, the Son of Man, God's gift of the Son to the world, light and darkness, and so on.

We are not told how Nicodemus received Jesus' theological discourse. It is very likely that he disappeared into the night from which he came, more confused than he was when he first approached Jesus. The story, however, does not end in the dead of night. The fact that Nicodemus reappears again during the day to defend Jesus and his ministry (John 7:50-52) and to accord him a befitting burial (John 19:39-42) offers a reassuring sign that their nocturnal theological conversation was probably not a futile exercise. Nicodemus is the model of a believer seeking a deeper understanding of his or her faith.

The second story comes from the Gospel of Luke 18:18-25. It is the story of the rich young man. Unlike the wise old Nicodemus, this man is not named. As the story unfolds, we know that he was very rich and a believer in God. He was also very conversant with the Ten Commandments of Moses, and he was eager to show off his knowledge and observance of the law. By the time the conversation is over, he is less enthusiastic and not as self-confident as he was when he first began to question Jesus. What was he seeking? He knew the provisions of the Law of Moses, but he wanted to find out what "to do" in order to inherit eternal life and be saved. Somehow, he had already resolved the question of understanding his faith. He was at the level of practical and concrete ways of living and loving as a believer. This rich young believer offers us an example of a kind of faith seeking love, a believer in search of right action and conduct. I will call this "faith seeking love."

The third and final story comes from the Gospel of Matthew. The central character of the story in Matthew 20:20-23 is the unnamed mother of James and John, two of Jesus' disciples. She appears as a typical African mother who knows what is good for her two boys and appears determined to make sure that the teacher offers them the best possible deal for their service to him. In Africa, she would be identified by her proper maternal status as "Mama James," that is, the mother of James, assuming that James was the older of the two.

Picture the image of this mother: she has just been informed by her two boys that there is a substantial reward attached to following Jesus of Nazareth. But it is a competitive world, and the other followers might succeed in negotiating better rewards than James and John. "Leave it to me," Mama James replies. "I'll take care of this." Off she goes, like an African mother, her head scarf tightly fastened around her waist to secure her wrapper, and her two would-be princes of the kingdom of heaven in tow. Who would dare refuse the request of this determined mother? Surprisingly, when they get to the place where Jesus is, she approaches him in a more humble manner but does not mince her words: "Tell me, preacher man, I mean, promise me. . . ." James and John and their mother are believers, but what can they hope for at the end of all their tedious labors and bruising journeys with Jesus? After all, they are abandoning their thriving trade as fishermen to follow Jesus. What is in this for them? Is this venture worth all the trouble that it entails? I would call this an example of "faith seeking hope."

Christianity's famous philosopher and theologian St. Anselm of Canterbury (1033-1109) gave us a definition of theology that has withstood the test of time. When confronted with the task of defining theology, he simply stated that it is "faith seeking understanding." He lived at a time when human reason dominated all matters concerning the faith. Understanding was most important. Yet, on the evidence of scripture, faith never stands alone; faith is never satisfied with merely understanding. In the words of Paul, faith stands with and seeks love and hope (1 Corinthians 13:13).

So let us ask the question again: What is theology? We can formulate an answer based on these three Gospel stories. I define theology as faith seeking understanding, love, and hope. But how does it proceed?

Let us go back to the stories. One of the common features appears to be the use of questions: Nicodemus comes with a serious question, and Jesus replies with and raises even more serious questions. The rich young man opens his conversation with a question: "Good teacher, what must I do?" Jesus replies with a question: "Why do you call me good?" The mother's first statement on behalf of James and John is direct, but Jesus replies with a question, seeking further clarification of her demand. And so it goes back and forth: question and answer and then more questions. This suggests a very important dimension of how theology is done: questions are raised based on our experience in life in the light of our faith. We do this all the time in our ordinary experience. Some are casual: Why is it raining today in the middle of the dry season? Some are more profound and deal with issues of life and death: Why is there so much suffering, poverty, and misery in Africa? Has God forgotten Africa and Africans? Why is my wife barren? Why did my crop fail? What caused the death of my child? These questions cannot be content with simple yes-or-no answers. They touch us deeply. They form part of our ongoing quest as believers for the meaning and purpose of our existence. They are questions of faith seeking understanding, love, and hope.

The Path We'll Take

In the course of the next few chapters we will reflect on our faith, following the example of Jesus, Nicodemus, the rich young man, Mama James, Mr. Brown, and Chief Akunna. Their way of talking about God will be our own model for articulating and striving to understand the reality of God in our experience of faith. How will we proceed? Since theology has much to do with our life of faith, we will share reflections on questions, issues, and aspects related to our faith. These reflections will be informed by the use of scripture, texts from other people's reflections, and our own concrete experiences. The Bible, the Christian book of faith, serves as a guide for our talk about God. Ghanaian theologian Mercy Amba Oduyoye once described the Bible as an embodiment of the footprints of faith. According to Vatican Council II (1962-65), the Bible should be the very soul of any theology: it contains the Word of

God, about whom theologians and all Christians speak. The Bible reflects on our faith based on the experience of the people of God and the believing and worshiping community of Christians. It also constitutes the foundation of the main elements of our belief over many centuries. As an account of our faith and belief, the Bible offers us different examples of how particular faith communities articulate their faith seeking love and hope.

In our study of theology it is important to keep in mind three basic questions. First, what is the evidence from *scripture* as the Word of God and the book of our faith? Our aim is not to quote chapters and verses from the Bible to prove or support our positions but rather to refer to the Bible to learn from the experience of our ancestors in faith. How did they experience God? How did they express their experience in words and actions?

Second, what is the experience or *tradition* of the church? I anticipate that most readers are members of the community called church. This community has existed in various forms and traditions for over two thousand years. That is a long time to accumulate experience, customs, and ways of doing things. In Africa we respect age and associate wisdom with the passing of years. The wisdom of our community of faith forms a deep well of insights for our reflection on God and our faith today.

Third, how do the many aspects of our faith and belief relate to and inform our experience and vice versa? This third element really has to do with *context*, that is, our life situation or, if we live in Africa, our situation in life as *African Christians*. This situation may appear very simple, but in reality it is very complex, as we shall discover in the following chapters. There is a lot crammed into this situation, and we shall try to be attentive (sensitive) to it in the course of our reflection on our faith. My underlying assumption is that our African background has a lot to contribute to our faith seeking understanding, love, and hope. The same is undoubtedly true of other locations.

The method adopted in this book involves bringing all these elements to interact with one another to shed some light on our path and quest to understand our faith and to express it more clearly and concretely. In the end, we may not obtain everything we set out to get, like Mama James and her sons, or find all the answers to our questions, like Nicodemus. But at least we should not leave with our heads bowed in sadness and disappointment, like the rich young man.

About This Brew

The title of this book is an adaptation of Ghanaian director Kwaw Ansah's popular movie, *Love Brewed in African Pot*, which premiered in 1980. Perhaps not many readers will be familiar with it. But that is beside the point. Love, like theology, is not the exclusive possession of a particular religious people. Different people form different notions of love and express its meaning in a variety of ways. As one African proverb says, we all can see the moon from the back of our parents' houses. While there is a tendency to see theology as a Western academic discipline, Chief Akunna would dispute that. Recently I read David Ford's *Theology: A Very Short Introduction* (Oxford: Oxford University Press, 1999). Though an excellent scholarly work, it appeared to me rather bland, and left me deeply dissatisfied. It did not speak to my experience of talking about God and religion as an African. It probably could not, considering the nature of theology I have outlined above. A few years earlier I had read C. S. Song's *Theology from the Womb of Asia* (Maryknoll, N.Y.: Orbis Books, 1986). I found it stimulating, and it provided some inspiration for writing *Theology Brewed in an African Pot*.

I cherish my religious and cultural background as an Edo Christian born and raised in the ancient kingdom of Benin, in Nigeria. How do I integrate this heritage into my faith seeking understanding, love, and hope? How does it help me articulate what I believe, love, and hope about God and about myself? These questions provided part of the initial impetus for embarking on the writing of this book. Though there are many things we can agree on as central to theology as an academic discipline and as a Christian tradition, there are many things I can and ought to be able to perceive and express through the prism of my rich, diverse, and profound African religious and cultural heritage. Hence the title *Theology Brewed in an African Pot*.

The title of this book consciously alludes to another uniquely African experience. Let me explain. In many places in *Things Fall Apart*, Chinua Achebe talks about the importance of a special drink called palm-wine, which is tapped from the sap of a palm tree. This drink is used during every important social event, including weddings and communal feasts. At one wedding ceremony the suitor presented fifty pots of palm-wine to the bride's family: "The pots of wine stood in their midst. . . . Groups of four or five men sat round with a pot in their midst. . . . It was a great feast." Palm-wine also accompanies a variety of ritual celebrations. When the protagonist of *Things Fall Apart*, Okonkwo, transgressed one of the religious codes of the clan, "he took with him a pot of palm-wine" to the shrine of the earth goddess, on the orders of the chief priest, to appease her. Even on casual visits, like during the Week of Peace, palm-wine is drunk to offer hospitality and celebrate friendship.

In Benin City, my home, we drink palm-wine. There are many ways of drinking palm-wine. It can be fresh, when it is still sweet and smooth like coconut milk. At this stage it is popularly called *pamy*. If you are the strong type, you let the palm-wine sit for a day or two in order to ferment. Then revelers prefer to call it *tombo* liquor (or "Push me, I push you"). And a third type is possible by distilling the *tombo* liquor so that it becomes pure spirit. At this stage it is called *kain-kain* or *ogogoro*. Connoisseurs often claim that when you drink it you literally begin to see spirits. This third level is reserved only for daredevils.

I compare theology to the three stages of palm-wine. The introductory stage or level is fresh, sweet, and smooth, like *pamy*. This is theology for the people of God. With a bit of more experience and analysis, it reaches a second level, like *tombo* liquor. This is theology for professionals. Yet some theologians prefer to operate at a level of abstraction that is not easily accessible to ordinary Christians. Just like *ogogoro*, this third level is reserved for the more hardened and daring drinkers. Each stage represents a unique facet of theology.

I situate *Theology Brewed in an African Pot* at the first level of theological reflection. It offers neither sophisticated arguments nor complicated analyses of the different themes or content of Christian faith. It is not even a technical recipe for doing theology. This book offers an invitation to drink, savor, and celebrate theology in an African context. It is palm-wine theology—the kind that is brewed to be sweet, refreshing, and enjoyable.

As may already be obvious, to serve this special brew of theology to readers, I have chosen an unusual instrument. I mentioned three key references above: *experience* (because of my experience as a convert to Catholicism), the *tradition* of the community called church, where we do theology, and the *Bible*, the Christian book of faith. But I have added another important reference to these three: Chinua Achebe's novel, *Things Fall Apart*. In my opinion, no other African novel matches the power, fascination, and brilliance of this literary masterpiece, which has sold more than ten million copies around the world and has been translated into fifty languages. What I have found intriguing in reading and rereading this novel is the fact that it contains such a profound source of wisdom, narratives, and events that can enrich, structure, and enlighten theological reflection from an African perspective. More significantly, this captivating African story provides me with an accessible methodology for giving theological reflection a distinctively African flavor. I recommend that readers of *Theology Brewed in an African Pot* also read *Things Fall Apart*.

First published in 1959, *Things Fall Apart* narrates the tragic story of Okonkwo, a man whose morbid fear of failure fired his obsessive quest for power, success, and fame. The story climaxes in the cataclysmic falling apart of his world. Religion appears as the catalyst. Okonkwo, it seems, was destined to be the sacrificial lamb for the titanic clash of two religious worlds: African and Christian. This simple novel presents a literary account of the conflict-ridden encounter between missionary Christianity and African religious and cultural worldviews in a way that has enduring significance, not only in African literature, but also in the study of religion and theology from an African perspective.

In addition, I have interspersed the chapters of this book with a collection of prayers. Over the years I have tried to shape my oral prayers into written form. I have just defined theology as faith in search of understanding, love, and hope. The unique place for this search to happen is within a community of believers. Not just any kind of community but a community of *praying, worshiping, and praising believers.* My theology feeds my life of prayer, praise, and worship and they in turn feed my theology. This suggests that we expand further the definition of theology: it is "faith seeking understanding, love, hope, prayer, praise, and worship." These prayers form part of my way of worshiping and my way of talking about God as an African. Perhaps they will spur the readers to reflect more deeply, not only on their own way of doing theology from an African perspective but also about their own way of praying, worshiping, and praising God as Africans, Europeans, Asians, and Americans.

Finally, the aspects of our faith that theology deals with are varied and wide. The implication of this is that we need to be selective, since one cannot hope to cover all the areas in such a small book. Given these factors, in the following chapters I will concentrate on the following "articles" of our faith: God, Trinity, creation, grace and sin, Jesus Christ, church, Mary, communion of saints, inculturation, and spirituality.

As I mentioned above, *Theology Brewed in an African Pot* presents an invitation to taste theology in an African context. The eleven short chapters of this book offer readers only a small and quick sip of theology brewed in an African pot. They are introductory in nature. My hope is that besides whetting the reader's appetite, they will stimulate his or her imagination and quest for a sensible way of talking about God and the Christian faith in whatever cultural setting he or she happens to be placed.

Enjoy this brew and the journey of faith seeking understanding, love, and hope in an African context.

Questions for Reflection and Group Discussion

1. Read the story of Jesus and the Samaritan woman at the well (John 4:1-42). What are some of the elements in this story that tell

us about the meaning of theology as the study of God and our word about God?

2. What do you consider to be the most important questions of faith and belief in today's world?

3. As a Christian, how does your faith in God help you to live a life of love and hope?

—⟲—

To the God of My Ancestors: Luke 17: 25, 27

When Jesus alludes to the difficulty of threading a camel's head through the eye of a needle, I immediately recognize the action of a dependable, personal, and mystery-working God who makes possible the impossible, of whom my ancestors spoke.

Mystery-working God,
You who poured milk into the coconut without opening
  its shell,
    may your word find a way in, even when
    stubbornness shuts the door to my heart.
You who planted the banana tree without the help of
  a seed,
    may your blessing germinate in my life, even when
    hardness of heart makes the soil infertile.
You who divided the kola-nut without splitting apart
  its lobes,
    may evil thoughts and malicious intentions vanish
    from my heart without leaving a trace.
Amen!

2

A "New God" Comes to Mbanta

At the climax of a particularly turbulent and traumatic encounter with God, Job confesses his ignorance of the nature and dealings of God with humility and satisfaction:

> I know that you can do all things, and that no purpose of yours can be thwarted. "Who is this that hides counsel without knowledge?" Therefore I have uttered what I did not understand, things too wonderful for me, which I did not know. "Hear, and I will speak; I will question you, and you declare to me." I had heard of you by the hearing of the ear, but now my eye sees you; therefore I despise myself, and repent in dust and ashes. (Job 42:2-6)

One of the most heated and controversial debates in the history of Western Christianity concerns the question of the nature and existence of God: Does God exist? How can we prove or disprove God's existence? What or who is God? Philosophers and theologians of ancient and medieval periods generated volumes of arguments for and against the existence of God, with varying degrees of success. Some were brilliant, others plain ridiculous. Even in our time we have not been indifferent to this debate. It is not confined to the circle of academic scholarship where experts of various stripes hold court over the reality or nonsense of God. Oftentimes the debate turns up in the unlikeliest of places.

A few years ago I came across an issue of *Newsweek* magazine with a bold and provocative headline adorning its cover: *Is God Dead? In Western Europe, it sure can look that way.* The magazine featured an article by Karen Armstrong, the author of *A History of God*, titled, "Where Has God Gone?" The author revisits nineteenth-century philosopher Friedrich Nietzsche's proclamation of the death of God and argues that God is still a relevant question for Europeans. The only difference between then and now, continues the author, lies in the fact that present generations of Europeans now find God elsewhere: art, rock music, lethal drugs, video games, and so on. Armstrong writes: "If the God of classical Western theism is dead for a large proportion of the population, this simply means that, once again, we are undergoing a period of religious transition. Even in post-Christian Europe, the quest for ecstasy continues, with or without God. We are so constituted that when one source of transcendent experience dries up, we simply seek it elsewhere."

In a similar vein, in June 2003, the international news magazine, *Time*, did a special report on Christianity in Europe. Its cover in red, bold letters read: *WHERE DID GOD GO?*

In a way, Armstrong implies that we cannot live without God. God is so important for who we are that, if God did not exist, we will have to create God. And we can change gods, as we do our clothes, depending on whether or not God fits our needs. This kind of reasoning gives much to reflect about. So, who or what is God?

My own presupposition is that the question of God's existence does not constitute a "burning question" for us as Africans. Philosophers, sociologists, anthropologists, and theologians who have studied various aspects of cultural and religious life in Africa never tire of reminding us that religion runs deep in the veins of Africans. They say Africans are notoriously and incurably religious. In other words, to adapt Armstrong's idea to our own situation, as Africans we cannot live without God.

In the previous chapter, I mentioned the complexity of the African situation. As Africans we are not just Christians, we are *African* Christians. We have embraced Christianity as our path to God and our way to live. And so we make a public statement of this option by making a profession of faith: "We believe in God!" For us, then, God exists; God is. Or, as we say in West African pidgin, *God dey!* Many public and commercial service vehicles in Africa carry this expression of faith about towns, cities, and villages in bright colors.

I do not intend to make the vexing question of God's existence or nonexistence the starting point of our reflection on God. If you think this assumption does not adequately express your situation in life, read no further. This book is not for you. If you choose to continue reading, then I have presumed correctly. You believe in God, who has communicated or manifested the divine being to us in the life, death, and resurrection (the paschal mystery) of Jesus Christ. This is our point of departure which in no way precludes our sincere desire and genuine effort to come to a better understanding of God in whom we have put our faith and trust (2 Tim 1:12).

The evidence we have from scripture is quite clear on the existence and nature of God (see, for example, Deut 6:4-5; Isa 45:22-24). If the contrary were the case, then we would not be talking about scripture. The Bible is an account of such faith in the existence and self-manifestation of God. To put it quite simply, the Bible is a book of faith that affirms the truth of God's existence. According to the Bible, "God is," *God dey!*

God the Communicator

The evidence from scripture does not stop at merely affirming the existence of God. It also tells us that God communicates with God's people. The act of communication, among other things, contains both a means and a message. The Letter to the Hebrews talks about God communicating with "our ancestors" at various times in history through various ways, means, and people (1:1). In theological language, this experience of God communicating the very being of God to us humans is called *revelation*. The experience of revelation or self-communication implies that God entered into a *relationship* with our ancestors in faith. The people of the Old Testament understood God as the God of covenant. This God made a formal pact or agreement with the people. God made a public commitment to the people, and the people in turn committed themselves to God. The terms of this agreement are summarized in one simple sentence: "I will be your God, and you shall be my people" (Lev 26:12; Jer 7:23; 11:4; 30:22; Ezek 36:28). But it does not end with the people of the Old Testament. In the New Testament, the promise that God made with our ancestors is fully fulfilled in the coming, life, death, and resurrection of Jesus Christ. To this day, God continues to communicate with us.

What does God communicate to us as the people of God? The answer is simple: God communicates or manifests *God's self* to us. Before anything else, God's primary interest and desire is to reveal to us who God is. Therefore, we can say that the very object of God's communication is *God's own self.* In the New Testament this self-communication will be experienced as Jesus Christ, the Word of God made flesh (John 1:14). God does not communicate another being or reality. God is not a messenger of another supreme being. God is the means and message of God's own act of communication. This is an important lesson for us to retain. Very often when we talk of revelation we think of the information and news that has been communicated to us by God. When a preacher, prophet, or priest tells us that God has revealed something to him or her, we immediately think of what new information we might have from God. Revelation is not the monopoly of preachers, prophets, pastors, and priests. As the Psalmist sings: "All the ends of the earth have seen the glory of God!" There is no exception.

The evidence from the Bible also points to the fact that God is revealed to us under different names. These names, as God reveals them in the Bible, tell us what God does in human life. God gives (and is) life, mercy, truth, light, love, freedom. To have a name means a lot to us Africans. Naming a child in Africa carries a lot of significance. In many parts of Africa the occasion of the naming of a child is a festive one. A person who has no name does not exist. There is a young Kenyan musician who goes by the name *Nameless.* But that is his stage name; his real name is David Mathenge. Among the Yoruba people of West Africa, some people are called *Kolorunko,* which means "I have no name." Among the Edo people of Benin City, some are called *Umweni,* which means "You have no name." In reality these statements are not entirely true, for as the

African proverb goes, "the name of a person who says 'I have no name' is 'I have no name'"!

In Africa a person's name is the carrier of hope for his or her future. Our names oftentimes tell of the experiences of our parents, families, clans, ancestors, and so on. On some occasions names tell a whole story about the circumstances of a child's birth. We see a clear example of this in the tragic story of Okonkwo's second wife, Ekwefi, in *Things Fall Apart*. Nine of her ten children died in infancy:

> Her deepening despair found expression in the names she gave her children. One of them was a pathetic cry, Onwumbiko—"Death, I implore you." But death took no notice; Onwumbiko died in his fifteenth month. The next child was a girl, Ozoemena—"May it not happen again." She died in her eleventh month, and two others after her. Ekwefi then became defiant and called her next child Onwuma—"Death may please himself." And he did.

Names confer identity and personality on us and allow for the possibility of entering into a relationship with other people, other names. God reveals the divine names so that we too might know God *as a personal God*, and call God by name, just as God calls us by name. One of the key implications of professing faith in God is that it involves a personal commitment. The declaration "God is" does not merely announce the logical conclusion to a brilliantly crafted theological or philosophical argument. To say "God is" implies to know, love, and worship God.

Our ancestors in faith encountered God, not as a nameless, faceless, and vague reality, but as the living God, who was, is, and will be. When Moses asked God to identify God's self by a personal name, God replied: "I AM WHO I AM. . . . This is my name forever, and this my title for all generations" (Exod 3:1-15).

What about African Christians: who is God for Africans? How do Africans address God? By what name has God been revealed to Africans?

God Has No Name and Many Names

Let us begin this part of our reflection with a selection from Chinua Achebe's *Things Fall Apart*. This part of the story recounts one of the first events in the encounter between missionary Christianity and African traditional religion in the village of Mbanta, where the major character in the story has fled into exile.

> The arrival of the missionaries had caused a considerable stir in the village of Mbanta. There were six of them and one was a white man. Every man and woman came out to see the white man. . . .
>
> When they had all gathered, the white man began to speak to them. . . . And he told them about this new God, the Creator of all the world and all the men and women. He told them that they worshipped false gods, gods of wood and stone. A deep murmur went through the crowd when he said this. He told them that the true God lived on high and that all men when they died went before Him for judgment. Evil men and all the heathen who in their blindness bowed to wood and stone were thrown into a fire that burned like palm-oil. But good men who worshipped the true God lived forever in His happy kingdom. "We have been sent by this great God to ask you to leave your wicked ways and false gods and turn to Him so that you may be saved when you die," he said. . . .
>
> At this point an old man said he had a question. "Which is this god of yours," he asked, "the goddess of the earth, the god of the sky, Amadiora or the thunderbolt, or what?"
>
> The interpreter spoke to the white man and he immediately gave his answer. "All the gods you have named are not gods at all. They are gods of deceit who tell you to kill your fellows and destroy innocent children. There is only one true God and He has the earth, the sky, you and me and all of us."
>
> "If we leave our gods and follow your god," asked

another man, "who will protect us from the anger of our neglected gods and ancestors?"

"Your gods are not alive and cannot do you any harm," replied the white man. "They are pieces of wood and stone."

When this was interpreted to the men of Mbanta they broke into derisive laughter. These men must be mad, they said to themselves. How else could they say that Ani and Amadiora were harmless? And Idemili and Ogwugwu too? And some of them began to go away.

Not a few people would find in this story evidence of missionary hubris, one that is extremely offensive. The novel's main character, Okonkwo, fought against it to the point of a violent confrontation that cost him his life and the soul of his people. One is tempted to think that things have changed since then. Contemporary theology is more sensitive to the religious sensibilities of non-Christians. That is not to say that fundamentalist evangelical Christianity has completely overcome its religious superiority complex on the question of "the true God" and "gods of wood and stone." It is a question that theology seeks to confront without alienating or antagonizing non-Christians.

As I mentioned at the beginning of this chapter, the question of God (or God-talk) in African religion and spirituality is not a controversial one. According to John Mbiti, who has written a lot about how Africans encounter, understand, and worship God, "All African peoples believe in God. They take this belief for granted." I completely agree with Mbiti. Wherever one chooses to look for evidence, in spite of the white man's declaration to the people of Mbanta, the belief in God is native to Africa. God is not a stranger to Africans. There is abundant and irrefutable evidence of various and different African conceptions of the reality called God. Not surprisingly, these conceptions may not be the same as the Western ideas of God, but they remain invaluable for an interpretation and understanding of God in African Christianity and any attempt to talk about God, that is, to do theology in Africa.

I suggest that if we are interested in knowing what Africans believe about God, we should look at three sources that are native to Africa: proverbs, songs, and names bearing "God," that is, theophoric names. In chapter 1 we saw an example of this when Chief Akunna reminded Mr. Brown that his ancestors knew God as the Supreme Being to the extent of representing this notion of God in the names given to their children: Chukwuka—"Chukwu is supreme."

Here is a sample of African proverbs that provide a window of insight on God's existence and nature from an African perspective:

+ God arranges things so that a leper's sandals fall apart under the camel-foot shrub, which provides the rope to mend them (Ghana).
+ God exercises vengeance in silence (Burundi and Rwanda).
+ God goes above any shield (Rwanda).
+ God is never in a hurry, but is always there at the right time (Ethiopia).
+ God knows the things of tomorrow (Burundi).
+ God saves the afflicted according to God's will (Uganda).
+ God drives away flies from the back of a tailless cow (Nigeria).
+ If God dishes you rice in a basket, do not wish to eat soup (Sierra Leone).
+ If God gives you a cup of wine and an evil-minded person kicks it over, God fills it up for you again (Ghana).
+ No one shows a child the Supreme Being (Ghana).
+ The one whom God clothes will never go naked (Ethiopia).
+ The stick of God does not cause one to cry (that is, it is not painful) (Kenya).
+ The plant protected by God is never hurt by the wind (Rwanda).
+ We do not see God; we see only the works of God (Ethiopia).

The Nupe (northern Nigeria) have a song that celebrates the creation of the world by the Supreme Being, Soko: "A being which

Soko did not create, neither did the world create it. . . . Should you do anything that is beautiful, Soko has caused it to be beautiful; should you do anything evil, Soko has caused it to be evil."

As for theophoric names, the examples from across Africa are infinite. Each one of these names makes a theological statement about God. The following is a short sample:

- Edo/Benin (Nigeria): *Osarugue* (God is my shield), *Osasere* (God is the greatest), *Igbinosa* (I take refuge in God), *Osaretinmwen* (God is my strength).
- Malagasy (Madagascar): *Rakotonomenjanahary* (the man given by God), *Andrianomenjanahary* (the prince given by God).
- Runyoro (Uganda): *Busobozibwaruhanga* (the power of God), *Ruhangamugabi* (God is the giver), *Karuhanga* (the child of God).
- Shona (Zimbabwe): *Ngonidzashe* (mercy of God), *Kudakwashe* (God's will), *Munashe* (with God).
- Kirundi (Burundi)/Kinyarwanda (Rwanda): *Havyarimana* (it is God who gives birth), *Birikumana* (everything depends on God), *Manirabona* (God sees/God watches).
- Igbo (Nigeria): *Chijioke* (God holds my portion of life), *Chinonso* (God is near/close by), *Chikaebere* (God is most merciful).

These names tell of God's nature and attribute particular qualities and functions to God. They describe in a succinct manner the various ways in which God relates to human beings—to give life, save, protect, guide, empower, and so on.

These African ways of speaking about God show us that Africans live in a religiously charged, even supercharged, environment. The African religious universe is populated by numerous gods, goddesses, divinities, deities, spirit beings, and ancestors. But this does not obscure the belief in one Supreme Being, whose eternal will holds sway over the destiny of all creation. Different African languages and cultures have different names for this Supreme Being: *Olodumare* (Yoruba), *Chukwu* (Igbo), *Osanobua* (Edo/

Benin), *Mungu* (Swahili), *Unkulunkulu* (Zulu), *Sikabumba* (Tonga), *Nzambi* (Kikongo), *Onyankopon* (Ashanti), *Zanahary* (Malagasy), *Ruhanga* (Runyoro), *Imana* (Kirundi/Kinyarwanda), and so on.

According to various African beliefs, the relationship between this Supreme Being and the other divinities is ordered in such a way that the (minor) gods and goddesses act as intermediaries between human beings and the one Supreme Being, God. As the Yoruba say:

> Be there one thousand four hundred divinities of the
> home;
> Be there one thousand two hundred divinities of the
> marketplace;
> Yet there is not one divinity to compare with Olodumare:
> Olodumare is the King Unique.

Belief in this God has strong moral implications for human beings in their daily existence, both individually and communally.

Characteristically, God in African religious expressions is a boundless Supreme Being who presides over the whole of the universe. This God is without boundaries. For Africans, God is everywhere. We encounter God everywhere. God is not indifferent to the affairs of the world. The proverbs and the theophoric names quoted above are very explicit about the various concrete roles that God assumes in our daily and ordinary experience and existence. God is neither indifferent to nor remote from the affairs of the world. God creates the universe and everything that exists, as the Nupe sing. There are gods, divinities, deities, and spirits who have some powers to act, but when it comes to creation, life is the gift of the Supreme Being who alone gives life.

Furthermore, the Supreme Being remains in constant communication and relationship with human beings, as I have indicated above while talking about revelation. How we represent God or the image we form of God depends on the roles we assign to God. Sometimes God is compared to a parent, a farmer, a warrior, a king, an artist, or a musician. In Africa, the names of God are as varied as people's experiences of God.

Given the above, one would expect the ways in which Africans understand and talk about God to vary from place to place. One thing remains indisputable: as Africans we believe that God exists. "God is." *God dey.* And according to the Swahili-speaking people of eastern Africa, *Mungu ni Mungu*—"God is God"!

Questions for Reflection and Group Discussion

1. In your own opinion is there any similarity between how God is understood in the Bible and how Africans understand and talk about God?

2. Identify and translate one or two names of God in your mother tongue. What is the literal meaning of these names? What do they say about who God is and what God does?

3. Based on your experience as a Christian, what names of God revealed in the Bible appeal most to you and why?

—⊖—

An African Invocation of Divine Names

Ancient deity,
Unbreakable stone,
Consoler and comforter providing salvation,
Grandfather who alone is the great one,
Watcher of everything who is not surprised by
    anything,
Piler of rocks into towering mountains,
Divider of night and day,
Response: We praise You!

Sun too bright for our gaze,
Eye of the sun,
Artist-in-chief,

Drummer of life,
Owner of our head,
Large and deep pot,
My feathered one,
Mother of people,
Response: Bless us!

Great nursing mother,
Great eye,
Great rainbow,
Great personal guardian spirit,
Unsurpassed great spirit,
Great source of being,
Great mantle which covers us,
Great leopard with its own forest,
Great healer of eternal life,
Great water-giver,
Great well,
Greatest of friends,
Great spider, the all-wise one,
Response: Enlighten us!

Controller of destiny in the universe,
All-powerful, never defeated,
Father of laughter,
King without blemish,
Possessor of whiteness,
Whiteness without patterns,
Caller-forth of the branching trees,
Unique great one to whom one can take
        petitions and requests for counsel,
Response: Hear us!

The first who always existed and will never die,
The only one bull in the world,
The one who sees both the inside and
    the outside,
The one we meet everywhere,
The one who is in all ages, everywhere and
    at all times,
The one who turns things upside down,
The one who has power to destroy completely,
The one who makes the sun set,
The one who gave everything on this earth and
    can take everything away,
Response: Guide us!

Axe that fears no thistle,
Hoe that fears no soil,
Ram of majestic sinews and majestic
    carriage,
Hero who never flees before the enemy,
Big boundless hut,
Victor over death,
Response: Protect us!

Compiled from John Mbiti, Introduction to African Religion *(London: Heinemann, 1975); Robert E. Hood,* Must God Remain Greek? Afro Cultures and God-Talk *(Minneapolis: Fortress Press, 1990); Joseph Healey and Donald Sybertz,* Towards an African Narrative Theology *(Maryknoll, N.Y.: Orbis Books, 1996), and other sources.*

3

The Mad Preacher and the Three Persons in One God

Glory be to the Father, the Creator and Source,
to the Nursing Mother,
to Jesus, the Healer and Eldest Brother
And to the Unsurpassed Great Spirit. Amen.

> East African Prayer, quoted in Joseph Healey,
> *Once Upon a Time in Africa: Stories of Wisdom
> and Joy* (Maryknoll, N.Y: Orbis Books,
> 2004), 128

The novel *Things Fall Apart*, by Nigerian writer Chinua Achebe, remains a great classic of African literature. As I mentioned in chapter 1, the central theme explored in this riveting story is the encounter between the African way of life, in its native beauty and earthy innocence, and missionary Christianity, with its disruptive intrusion and baggage of bewildering concepts and doctrines of religion. In one scene, a missionary struggles to explain what appears to his audience as a ludicrous notion of three persons in one God.

> After the singing the interpreter spoke about the Son of God whose name was Jesu Kristi. Okonkwo, who only stayed in the hope that it might come to chasing the men out of the village or whipping them, now said:
> "You told us with your own mouth that there was only one god. Now you talk about his son. He must have a wife then." The crowd agreed.

26

"I did not say He had a wife," said the interpreter, somewhat lamely.

"Your buttocks said he had a son," said the joker. "So he must have a wife and all of them must have buttocks."

The missionary ignored him and went on to talk about the Holy Trinity. At the end of it Okonkwo was fully convinced that the man was mad. He shrugged his shoulders and went away to tap his afternoon palm-wine.

Who could blame Okonkwo for failing to comprehend this new and seemingly bizarre understanding of God as Holy Trinity? The Christian understanding, experience, and belief in God are Trinitarian. Christianity traditionally represents the nature of God as Father, Son, and Spirit. It is hard enough to explain it to Christians, let alone explaining it clearly to the people of Umuofia village. This Christian understanding is a unique notion, and quite unlike our African conceptions of God.

As a convert to Catholicism, one of the questions I had to answer during catechetical instruction was "How many persons are there in one God?" The response was as simple as a mathematical answer: "There are three persons in one God: God the Father, God the Son, and God the Holy Spirit." "Are there three Gods?" continued the catechist. "No, there are three persons in *one* God." As long as I parroted the correct formula, I could be promoted to the rank of a full member of the Catholic Church. But what did I really understand? To explain this baffling theological equation the catechist complicated the situation further by resorting to arithmetical formulas that he would scribble on the chalkboard: God + God + God = God! Or $1 + 1 + 1 = 1$. The end result? A young catechumen, like myself at the time, was left in a confused state. I conveniently shrugged off the problem, like Okonkwo, who preferred the pleasure of his afternoon palm-wine to the lame attempt by the missionary to explain the madness of the Triune God. After all, the Trinity is a mystery; why bother to understand it? Yet I knew the catechist was wrong in the way he tried to initiate us into the madness of the three persons in one God.

The doctrine of the Triune God is not an abstract numerical

puzzle. The question it should confront us with is not "How come 1 + 1 + 1 = 1?" Instead, we should ask: What does it tell us about God's relationship with us? How do we understand this relationship? Viewing the Trinity as a mathematical puzzle inadvertently leads to tri-theism. This approach fails to articulate the reality that God is one, that God is fullness, and that God is present to us. Our point of departure is to understand Trinity as a *symbol*, not a road map into the inner workings of the divinity.

A symbol points the way and allows us the possibility of expanding our horizon of thought; it does not pretend to contain everything that it attempts to represent. Like all symbols, Trinity points beyond itself to something larger and fuller than our imagination can comprehend. It does not block the way to understanding; rather, it opens the way to an experience of reality in a much deeper and personal way. In this case, the symbol of the Trinity points to the event and nature of our salvation. It reminds us that we are saved by God, through Jesus Christ, in the power of the Holy Spirit. The Letter to the Ephesians (1:3-14) summarizes this truth very eloquently. It begins by cataloging all the spiritual blessings from God since the creation of the world and how all of them find fulfillment in the life, death, and resurrection of Jesus Christ, and, finally, how everything is sealed and sanctified in the gift and outpouring of the Holy Spirit. There is one movement that unfolds and washes over us simultaneously as creation in God, redemption in Christ, and sanctification by the Holy Spirit. It has everything to do with a living and saving relationship with the God of life, and little if anything to do with arithmetic.

Trinity is our unique way as Christians of speaking about God and what God has done and continues to do in our lives. God is revealed to us through and in Christ. Vatican Council II's document *Dei Verbum* tells us, "The most intimate truth thus revealed about God and human salvation shines forth for us in Christ, who is himself both the mediator and the sum total of revelation" (no. 2). Trinity is not separate from our salvation in Christ. We know God as Father, Son, and Spirit only because Jesus came to save us in the power of the Spirit and show us the way to God (see John 14).

Oftentimes, some people use quotations from the Bible as proof texts for the doctrine of the Holy Trinity. Some quote, for example, Genesis 1:26; 11:7; and Isaiah 6. Looking for and claiming to find the doctrine of the Triune God in the Bible is something we need to be extremely careful about. Texts from the Bible may enlighten our Trinitarian faith, but they do not contain a doctrine of the Holy Trinity. This doctrine was developed much later, mainly in the fourth century c.e. It is true that we find quite a few very explicit texts in the New Testament that contain "Trinitarian formulas." Although these texts are more explicit in their reference to the Triune God, this should not be confused with a developed doctrine of the Holy Trinity. Some theologians used these texts to support this doctrine during the great Trinitarian controversies of the fourth century.

A sample of these texts shows that some are "binitarian" (referring to Father and Son, Son and Spirit, or Father and Spirit), for example, Ephesians 5:20; Romans 4:24; 8:11; 2 Corinthians 4:14; Colossians 2:12; 1 Timothy 2:5; 6:13; and 2 Timothy 4:1. Other texts make reference to a tri-relationship involving Father, Son, and Spirit: Matthew 28:19; 2 Corinthians 13:14; Matthew 3:16-17; Galatians 4:6; Romans 8:14-17; Ephesians 1:3-14; 1 Corinthians 6:11; 12:4-6; 2 Corinthians 1:21-22; 1 Thessalonians 5:18-19; and Galatians 3:11-14.

The common feature of the majority of these texts is that they were used by our ancestors in faith as short formulas that summarize the key elements of the Christian faith, such as belief in "the God and the Father of our Lord Jesus Christ" (Rom 15:6; 2 Cor 1:3; Eph 1:3; and Col 1:3). But the most common context in which these references developed and were frequently used was that of the community gathered in prayer and worship. In other words, these references grew out of the liturgical life of the early Christian communities; they were not seminal Trinitarian doctrines containing all the jargon and technical language of the doctrine, as we know it today. This implies that while we can say that our current understanding of the Holy Trinity is biblical, it does not mean it was developed as such, that is, as a doctrine in the Bible.

Let me say a bit more about the idea of development. The doctrine of the Holy Trinity gradually came together as a clear teaching of the church at the time of what is now known in church history as the great Trinitarian heresies, mainly during the fourth century C.E. Along with the doctrine, theologians also created a terminology (language) for talking about the Trinity. Unfortunately, this language drew heavily on the dominant forms of abstract and speculative Greek philosophy, namely, neo-Platonism. Our ways of talking about the Triune God today bear the burden of this Greek legacy. Hence, it is little surprising that it is very technical, limited, and hardly adapted to the context and circumstances of today's Christians.

We need to keep in mind that the doctrine of the Holy Trinity emerged from the heated debates and controversies around some contested positions, many of which were subsequently declared to be heretical. To say the doctrine was "developed," however, does not amount to saying that the whole idea of God as Trinity is the product of the fertile imagination of theologians. Theologians did not create the idea of God as Trinity.

As I mentioned above, what is more evident in the New Testament is the liturgical usage of formulas referring to God as Father, Son, and Spirit. In this context, the community directs its praise, worship, and thanksgiving to God through Christ (Eph 5:20; 1 Cor 15:57; Col 3:17; Rom 1:8; 16:27). A clear example of how these texts appeared in the liturgical context is Matthew 28:19. Early Christians were baptized in the name of the Father, and of the Son, and of the Holy Spirit. Today, we have maintained this practice in our Christian tradition.

There is a question that remains to be asked in the context of African theology. As an African how do I understand the idea of the Triune God? Is there anything in my African background that gives me a unique insight into the meaning of three persons in one God? The answer is a categorical yes, and the rest of the chapter will be devoted to my understanding, as an African, of the Trinity. The earlier encounter with the catechist left me dissatisfied, just as Okonkwo's encounter with the missionary left him disappointed.

In the next section I shall use the image of an African mother as a metaphor or symbol for the Triune God.

Obirin Meta, *a Many-Sided Character*

In Nigeria, the Yoruba people have a compound name for a special kind of woman: *Obirin meta*. *Obirin* means "woman," and *meta* means "three." When you put the two together, the name designates a woman who combines the strength, character, personality, and beauty of three women. *Obirin meta* is a woman with many sides, a many-sided character. She is a multifunctional woman of unmatched density and unbounded substance.

Anyone familiar with the daily struggles of life in Africa would have met such women at some point along the busy streets of Africa's bustling towns and cities or in the rugged paths of its hamlets and villages. I have met quite a few. I think of a mother who could balance a big pot of water or a basket of produce on her head, with a baby strapped to her back, trying to make it home on time to prepare dinner for the whole family, taking care of all the needs of the family, and being a mother to all. In the midst of all these tasks and chores she might even be carrying another baby in her womb. It takes a special kind of woman to do this—it takes *Obirin meta.*

I recall a unique sight on one of the busy streets of Lagos in Nigeria of a mother at the steering wheel of a car, struggling to negotiate the chaotic rush hour traffic with one hand and at the same time to breastfeed her baby firmly clasped to her bosom with the other hand. She cuts a striking image of *Obirin meta.*

Not long ago I saw a painting of a rather unusual scene in the dining room of a religious house of formation in Arusha, Tanzania. In the painting, christened *The Burden* by Ugandan Jesuit artist Kizito Busobozi, a pregnant woman is returning from the fields with bundles of produce and firewood piled high on her head, and a baby strapped to her back. In one hand she has a hoe, the instrument of her manual labor; the other hand is holding her load to prevent it from falling. The shocking part of the painting is the sight of a bearded man stooped in front of this heavily laden mother and suckling at her exposed right breast. We might say, "This can't be true! Grown men do not suckle." Yet, the artist's intention paints a very familiar reality in Africa: women take responsibility for the well-being of all members of the family, both young and old. Everybody depends on her strength, nurture, and hard labor—albeit sometimes to the point of exploitation—as the source and sustainer of life. This is a vivid image of *Obirin meta*.

Obirin meta does not simply describe someone from the outside, that is, by identifying material or physical traits and attributes. Beyond exterior qualities, it designates something deeper that forms the essence, substance, or core of the person, and how the many dimensions of her interior reality relate and interact to characterize her as a unique kind of woman. *Obirin meta* describes a woman who combines largeness of heart, strength of character, and depth of wisdom and insight.

Let us come back to the doctrine of the Triune God. This image of an African woman offers a unique way of understanding the reality called Trinity. How do we name God? How do we name God from the inside and from the outside? As I mentioned above, naming God is a contentious theological pastime with a long history. And one of the names we have settled for is Trinity, or three persons in the one God. But as soon as we name God in this way, we always run into difficulty, namely, how to understand the language and theology we have chosen for God. Sometimes, to avoid fighting over terminology and formulas, we settle for mystery; we say God is a mystery we cannot comprehend or understand. Oftentimes to settle for mystery is to settle for distance. Yet, our faith remains very clear about the desire of God to embrace us in the flesh and pitch tent in our midst (John 1:14).

The character called *Obirin meta* gives us a way to name and understand God without alienating ourselves from God or preferring to go and tap our afternoon palm-wine, like Okonkwo. Theologically, that is, talking about God, it would not be out of place to think of God using the symbol of *Obirin meta*. What would this kind of God look like? Not a majestic high God enrobed in terrifying inapproachable light. Rather, *Obirin meta* allows us to form the idea and open up to the experience of a God who combines many sides, many personalities, many realities, many relationships, and many qualities *at the same time and as the one and the same God.* Another way of putting it is to say that *Obirin meta* symbolizes the abundant and radical open-endedness of God in God's self and in our encounter of God.

The veil of mystery is lifted, and we are able to recognize the God who enters into our experiences and meets us where we are.

When I think of our African ways of naming God, this divine Trinitarian reality makes sense to me. Like *Obirin meta*, God is *unbreakable stone*, when we need God to be strong for us; the *eye that sees the four corners of the world*, when we are overwhelmed by the complexities of our existence; the *river that never ceases to flow*, when we need God to shower us with blessings; the *slender arm pregnant with kindness*, when we need God to be generous; the *deep pot*, when we need God's unfathomable wisdom to unravel the mysteries of life; the *great nursing mother*, when we need God's love like we have known that of a nursing mother. The list can go on. What we need to realize by naming God in this way is that the mystery blocking our imagination and understanding disappears. God comes closer to us in the reality of everyday living. There is no mystery here—only God who is all things to us, inside and outside, the radically open-ended One.

Our God, like the African *Obirin meta*, combines many sides. Christian revelation presents God as a hyphenated God, always showing us a surplus side in our attempt to understand and embrace the divine presence in our life. Our God is God-mother, -father, -son, -daughter, -brother, -sister, -friend, -lover, -consoler, -comforter, -creator, -redeemer, -sanctifier . . . *at the same time and as the one and the same God*. Trinity is the name we call God in our theological conversation, but many are the ways in which God meets us where we are, here and now, like *Obirin meta*. There is no mystery here.

The above Trinitarian symbol may not be complete or explain all the intricacies and complexities of God as Trinity. That is not the aim of appealing to this African maternal symbol. The underlying idea is that it is possible to gain an insight into the Trinitarian reality of God that is more refreshing than the missionary's awkward attempt, which Okonkwo easily dismissed as madness. Had the missionary told Okonkwo that God was like his mother, perhaps he would have considered putting off his afternoon quest for palm-wine in favor of understanding the closeness of God to him.

There is no limit to the symbols we might find and apply to the idea of the Trinity in Africa. One could think of the proverb that says that the cooking pot sits on three stones. The flame emanating from the fireplace made of three stones is one; so are the pot and the ultimate aim. But the stones maintain their individual identity while participating in the common task of cooking. Does this suggest something about God as Trinity? What about the round hut or *tukul* that one finds in many parts of rural Africa? There is always one main post that holds the entire edifice in place. This main post is distinct from the roof and the main wall, both of which also support the structure of the hut. Together they form a home, a place of gathering, of comfort, and of rest. Does this image conjure up something Trinitarian in our minds?

We only have to look. In Africa we are surrounded by countless Trinitarian symbols; they tell us that God is "the one we meet everywhere," "who sees both the inside and the outside."

Questions for Reflection and Group Discussion

1. How would you explain belief in the Trinity to a sixteen-year-old who is considering converting to Christianity?

2. Read the stories of creation in the book of Genesis: what are some of the qualities and attributes of God that the author(s) try to emphasize?

3. Traditionally we refer to God as Father, Son, and Spirit: can you identify other ways of naming God or other symbols for God from your experience of daily living that capture the same idea of God as Trinity?

A Prayer of Intercession

Gentle breeze from the four corners of the earth,
Bear our prayer on your wings to the court of the most
    high God.

Blazing sun, do not scorch our petition.

Falling rain, do not drown our request.

Flashing lightning, do not strike down our plea.

Roaring thunder, do not scare our supplication. . . .

Beaming moon, illumine our prayer before our God.

Twinkling stars, show our prayer the way to the abode
of God.

Gentle dew, water the path of our prayer to the
dwelling of God, the most high.

Rustling wind, make our prayer pleasing to the ears of
God.

Gentle breeze from the four corners of the earth,

Bear our prayer on your wings to the court of the most
high God.

*Inspired by John 3:8, and the African proverb, "If you want to speak to
God, tell it to the wind."*

Prayer for Light, Water, and Food

Introduction

Presider: O God, you are the creator and potter of the
universe and our world; you raised the hills and
the mountains to their lofty heights and dug the
valleys to surround them; you set the great lights
in the sky; you drew water from the bowels of the
earth, and provided abundant food for all your
creatures.

Presider: We pray for light.

Reader: The light of the risen Christ dispels the
darkness of our world. Remove from our midst the

plague of inefficiency that causes irregular power supply. We pray O Lord.

Presider: We pray for water.

Reader: The risen Christ gives us living water that wells up to everlasting life. Show us the way to utilize the abundant water resources you have blessed our world with for the good of our people. We pray O Lord.

Presider: We pray for food.

Reader: You send your rains to nourish the seeds that we sow, and to give us a rich and abundant harvest. Our land is fertile, yet so many of our brothers and sisters go without food. Help us to be self-sufficient in the production of food crops. We pray O Lord.

Presider: Let us pray to God who promised us to be the provider of our daily bread.

(*Conclude with the Lord's Prayer.*)

4

In the Beginning
There Were Many Stories

In the previous two chapters, I have focused our reflection on the question of God from the perspective of our Christian faith and African religious worldview. There we discovered that we cannot exhaust the reality of God by simply relying on a carefully crafted arithmetical formula. The Triune God transcends such formulas and yet relates to us as a many-sided God capable of being represented with many symbols. Even when we talk of God as Father, Son, and Spirit, we are using a symbol that approximates rather than circumscribes the interior and exterior reality of God. It creates a window on the question of who God is for us rather than casts the meaning of God in stone.

As I pointed out in chapter 1, the question of God lies at the heart of *theo*-logy. Theology is our reflection on *God-for-us*. This question, however, constitutes only one side of a larger question, the other half of which deals with human existence. Who are we? Why are we here? How did we get where we are? Where are we heading? Surrounded by the immensity and diversity of creation, we cannot but exclaim with the psalmist: "O LORD, our Sovereign, how majestic is your name in all the earth! . . . What are human beings that you are mindful of them, mortals that you care for them?" (Ps 8:1, 4; see Ps 104). These questions concern the origin and destiny or goal of creation.

The Christian statement of faith declares categorically that God is the creator of everything that exists. This statement relies on the evidence of scripture, though some theologians have always

37

maintained that it is enough for us to marvel at the intricate composition and configuration of our universe and conclude that God had a hand in how it came to be.

An African proverb says that if you do not know where you are going, you should at least know where you are coming from. As human beings we are fascinated by the origin of things. We want to know how we came to be, where we came from, and so on. How we answer this question of our origin is a serious affair. As I wrote this chapter, the BBC was reporting the news about a federal judge in the United States who ruled that the concept of the intervention at a determined time in the past of some higher power in the origin and development of the Earth cannot be taught in public schools. Proponents of this theory of "intelligent design" hoped to offer an alternative, first, to the theory of evolution (natural selection of species and survival of the fittest), which was originally propounded by Charles Darwin (1809-1882) and, second, to the belief in "creationism," which generally adopts a literal interpretation of the accounts of creation in Genesis. Accordingly, God created the universe and all it contains over a certain time frame and at a well-determined moment in history. They reject a natural explanation in favor of a supernatural explanation for unexplained natural phenomena. The judge, apparently, was not convinced, so he ruled that "intelligent design" is religious explanation masquerading as scientific theory, and it violated the First Amendment of the U.S. Constitution on the separation between church and state. The controversy continues to rage.

However we look at it, religion claims a significant stake in the ongoing debate on the origin of the universe. For us, it is a theological question worth exploring.

I shall take seriously the advice of the proverb quoted above and concentrate the focus of this chapter on the how and why of our creation.

In the preceding chapter I introduced the notion of development in relation to the doctrine of the Trinity. This notion also applies to the question of creation. The doctrine of creation was developed over many centuries by generations after generations of Christian thinkers and theologians. The process continues, but not without controversies and disagreements. The basic tenet of this doctrine is expressed in the Nicene Creed, which some Christians profess frequently and regularly at the celebration of the Eucharist as follows: "We believe in one God, the Father, the Almighty, creator of heaven and earth, of all that is seen and unseen." The faith expressed in this solemn declaration has a certain ring of absoluteness to it. In it we affirm three basic ideas. First, that, without exception, the whole of creation owes its origin to the will and action of God. We do not and cannot create ourselves; nothing in our entire universe has that capacity to will and execute its existence. God has a hand in the existence of everything that exists. Second, the whole of creation depends on God and makes sense only because of God. Finally, the ultimate purpose, goal, and destiny of creation lie in God. As the psalmist suggests above, creation stimulates us to make a proclamation of faith, because what we see in creation points beyond itself to the creator. We have some interesting texts on this question from the Bible:

> For all people who were ignorant of God were foolish by nature; and they were unable from the good things that are seen to know the one who exists, nor did they recognize the artisan while paying heed to his works. (Wis 13:1)

> For from the greatness and beauty of created things comes a corresponding perception of their Creator. (Wis 13:5)

Besides the basic affirmations contained in the statement of faith called the Creed, our Christian faith in God as creator comprises many aspects.

To begin with, there is only *one creator*. Creation does not happen through intermediaries or some lesser beings or gods. The Supreme Being is solely responsible for creation and holds absolute sway over all of creation. From a Christian perspective, and as suggested in the previous chapter, creation is an act of the Triune God. The creator calls forth creation by the Eternal Word, Jesus Christ ("through him all things were made"), and animates it by the Sanctifying Breath (Holy Spirit) (see Ezek 37:1-14).

Just as God does not depend on any other being or reality in order to create, so also *God does not need any preexisting material in order to create*. Traditionally, this understanding is expressed as creation *ex nihilo* ("creation out of nothing"). We need to be careful how we understand this formula. To say that God creates "out of nothing" amounts to making a statement about the meaning of God: God does not depend on any substance in order to create, and so creation does not derive from the substance of God. Nor is it a necessary emanation from God. Besides, God is greater than all created things, transcends all of creation, and does not depend on creation for divine existence. Thus, creation *ex nihilo* contains a powerful reminder that we owe our existence entirely to God's creative action.

Again, to recall my days as a catechumen preparing for reception into the church, during the class on creation the catechist would ask: "Who made you?" The response was brief and straight to the point: "God made me." "Why did God make you?" The honest answer would have been "I don't know!" An answer like that would have resulted in my instant disqualification as a candidate for the new faith. So, I would answer faithfully: "God made me to love God, to serve God, and to be happy with God forever in this world and in the world to come," as stipulated in the *Catechism*. This answer suggested a certain kind of necessity. As I understood it, God made me because God *needs* me to love God in return. Thus, creation appeared as a selfish act. God could do it, so God did it for God's sake. The truth is very different, even though the catechist did not quite grasp it. The ultimate end that God intends in creating us is our intimate participation in the life of God; creation is a loving, saving event. Therefore, many theologians would argue that God does not create out of a necessity; God does not seek to acquire or gain something for God's self by creating us other than the desire to generously and abundantly share with us the glory of the divine life. In other words, *God creates freely out of love*.

The image that comes to mind here is that of a boiling pot of okra sauce. As the proverb goes, a good okra sauce cannot be confined to the pot. Anyone who has seen okra being cooked in West Africa knows that it is in its nature to bubble over and overflow the cooking pot. It is its unique way of showing or manifesting its abundant goodness. This is an apt imagery for God's generosity, which overflows as creative, boundless love. It is in the nature of the okra to overflow abundantly. It belongs to the essence of God to overflow abundantly. There is no necessity, only love expressing itself without reservation, that explains our origin.

Another important implication of this affirmation is that creation is neither the result of blind fate nor a chance happening. It is freely willed by God.

Oftentimes we talk about *God's plan* for us or *divine providence*. As Christians, we believe we are in this world for a purpose. The purpose of creation is for good: "For surely I know the plans I have for you, says the LORD, plans for your welfare and not for harm, to give you a future with hope" (Jer 29:11). The belief that God has a divine plan for creation precludes falling into a kind of error known as *deism*, that is, the belief that God created the world but left it to its own devices (or fate) and does not interfere with the laws governing the universe. One of the most fundamental truths revealed in the Bible is God's continued involvement and relationship with all of God's creatures. God continues to care for, sustain, and guide all of creation. I alluded to this fact in the previous chapter. The Israelites of old expressed this relationship in the mode of covenant: "And I will walk among you, and will be your God, and you shall be my people" (Lev 26:12). In the New Testament, this relationship between God and creation takes flesh in Jesus Christ (John 1:14).

God's continued involvement in and guidance of creation toward its ultimate end does not rule out or suppress our human freedom to cooperate with or to even resist God's will. We know that God's divine plan or will is often obscured by evil in the world. Despite the presence of evil, our faith assures us that creation continues to *journey* toward a state of perfection in God (see 1 Cor 15:23-28).

Finally, in creation, the human person holds a place of preeminence. Only human beings know that they are created and strive to know and love their creator, in whose image they are created. As human beings, we are conscious of our *dignity, spiritual nature*, and the fundamental *equality* of all women and men.

Back in Time

Many books of the Bible talk about creation. We have already seen some key aspects of the doctrine of creation. This doctrine draws considerably on the evidence provided in the Bible. When we look at the evidence in the Bible concerning creation, however, we notice that it does not present a uniform view on the how and why of creation. To find out what the Bible says about creation, we have to sift through pages and pages of stories, creeds, hymns, poems, and so on that talk about God as creator of the world.

The most popular and influential biblical story of creation is the one that we find at the beginning of the Bible in the book of Genesis. We need to bear in mind that whatever is said about creation in the Bible has its origin in the faith of the author. That faith, like the creed we profess, simply affirms that *God is the creator of the universe and all that exists.*

Creation offers the biblical writers a way of talking about God: how God deals with or relates to the people of God. The focus and purpose of this way of talking about God are not necessarily scientific; they are based on faith. To affirm that God is creator the ancient writers use "contemporary" language, that is, the language of their own time. This language is more imaginative, poetic, and concrete than it is scientific, discursive, and speculative. Their intention was not to communicate a scientific truth, in the way that we have come to understand science in our own day and age. For example, the writers are not disturbed by the fact that two separate and apparently contradictory accounts of creation are given in Genesis. Let us take a brief look at this biblical expression of faith in the God of creation.

As I mentioned above, Genesis provides us with two accounts of creation, in 1:1-2:4a and 2:4b-24. The first account belongs to a much later period in the history of the Israelites (sixth century B.C.E.). It coincides roughly with the time of the Babylonian exile. It is set against the background of other competing accounts of how the world came to be. In general, the experience of exile introduced a lot of chaos into Israel's national life (religious, cultural, socio-economic, and political). The account of creation derived from this experience focused on God's *transcendence over chaos*. In the beginning, "the earth was a formless void and darkness covered the face of the deep," begins the story. Over a well-determined period of time, and taking some deliberate steps, God establishes order over the formless void for the people of God. God introduces *order* into what seems to be already in existence but in a visibly chaotic form: "In the beginning when God created the heavens and the earth, the earth was a formless void and darkness covered the face of the deep, while a wind from God swept over the face of the waters" (Gen 1:1-2).

The prevailing context and circumstances of life for the people of the Old Testament shaped their understanding of God as creator. During the time of their exile the Israelites encountered other stories of creation. According to some of these accounts of the origin of the universe, God succeeded in instilling order in the chaotic universe only after God or the creating agent had engaged in a protracted and often mortal struggle with several opposing forces of nature. It is only when these latter have been defeated (or their powers restrained or neutralized) that creation takes place. The Genesis account of creation paints a totally different picture of how creation happened "in the beginning."

To make creation happen or to instill order, God's *word* is absolutely sufficient. As I mentioned above, God does not need any other spiritual or cosmic power to create. The author of the first story of creation does not entertain any reservations regarding the commanding power and efficacy of God's word: "Then God said, 'Let there be light'; and there was light!" This account follows a temporal progression (of days), which culminates in the Sabbath, a day of worship and praise. This reveals something about how the writer understood the purpose of creation. As the Letter to the Ephesians would later formulate it, it was "so that we . . . might live for the praise of God's glory" (1:12). In this scheme of things, man and woman have a special relationship with God, and an important responsibility of stewardship for the works of God's hands.

In the second, shorter story, which belongs to the time of the monarchy (David-Solomon: tenth century B.C.E.), the emphasis is more on offering an explanation for *why things are the way they are.*

We should read it as a whole, that is, Genesis 2:4b-3:24. It affirms the goodness of God, the benevolent gardener who provides for the needs of all creation; the fundamental equality, mutuality, and interdependence of man and woman; and the advent of sin in the world because of human disobedience. Rather than command the universe into existence, God shapes and animates it into life in a very personal and deeply involving manner.

In addition to these Genesis texts, there are other texts in the Bible that present other views on creation-faith. Rather than dwell on these texts, I will proceed to look at some texts that talk about how we understand creation from an African perspective.

Stories from "Before Before"

I want to make two points in this section. First, African cultures pay particular attention to the question of origins. In some African languages, we have a historical time frame that is best translated into English as "before before." It is primordial time; no one in living memory recalls that time, but all carry a collective memory of the events that make up that time of "before before." As Africans, we tell in stories, songs, proverbs, and different forms of speech how we came to be where we are. These stories also form the basis of a creation-faith or faith in the creator of the universe. Second, African creation-faith may not, and need not, affirm the same things that our Christian faith affirms. The essential point is that, like the notion of God, the theology of creation is native to Africa. Unlike the foolish people "who were ignorant of God . . . were unable from the good things that are seen to know the one who exists, nor did they recognize the artisan while paying heed to his works" (Wis 13:1), Africans possess a lively, expansive faith that proceeds from the affirmation of creation and culminates in the proclamation of the existence of the creator.

So, let us look briefly at some African stories of creation that exist in a variety of oral traditions, collected in Harold Scheub's *A Dictionary of African Mythology: The Mythmaker as Storyteller* (New York: Oxford University Press, 2000).

Doondari was the creator. In the beginning, Doondari descended to the earth and created a stone, which created iron, which created fire, which created water, which created air. Doondari, having again descended to the earth, shaped those five elements into man. Because man was proud, Doondari created blindness. When blindness became too proud, Doondari overcame it by creating sleep. When sleep became too proud, Doondari created worry. When worry became too proud, Doondari created death. When death became too proud, Doondari descended a third time, and, as Gueno, the eternal one, he defeated death (Fulani/Mali and Senegal).

Kiumbi, the creator, created the ancestors and all things that they required. These ancestors became mediators between God the creator and the living members of society. Kiumbi had his dwelling place in the sky. Formerly Kiumbi had regular commerce with people. But the people disobeyed him, eating eggs that he had ordered them not to eat. They did this because they were cheated by a person whose name was Kiriamagi. As a result, God withdrew himself to a distant abode. Now the people were alone, without fellowship with God. But he sometimes visited them. People attempted to build a tower to reach God's place and thereby attain the former fellowship with him. But the higher they built, the farther God's place receded. Eventually, God punished the people with a severe famine, during which all the people died except two youths, a boy and a girl. All the people on earth descend from this pair. Since then, man's fellowship with God has been remote, and communication with him has to be sought with the ancestors who are closer to him than the living members of the society (Asu, Pare/Tanzania).

Chido, the supreme being, the sky god, the one who is above, also known as Ama or Ma, is identified with the celestial phenomena in general and with the sun in particular. Ama or Ma, the creator god, the earth god, is the fashioner of humans and of everything that lives and grows, and is also the lord of the underworld. Ama endows the corn with its nourishing qualities; Chido sends the rain and causes the corn to ripen. . . . Ama is the female counterpart of Chido—they are a father sky and a mother earth by whose union the crops and other living things are born. . . . Ama, creator of all living things, patron of childbirth, nourisher of crops, identified with the earth, queen of the underworld, sits before Chido, who is always present on earth, creating men and things. Ama created the world at early dawn. She (or he) made the firmament and holds it up. Ama is the earth: when a man dies he goes to Ama, for every living thing that dies, whether human, beast, or bird, returns to earth. She reigns in Kindo, the underworld, from which humans came, to which they all return, and from which they may return to earth a second time. She fashions the human body, bone by bone, as a potter builds up her pot strip by strip. When Ama has finished fashioning a man, Chido breathes life into his body, and for this purpose Chido descends to the earth. Similarly, Chido is the giver of grains to men, but it is Ama who fashions it. She is the earth, which is fertilized by Chido in the form of rain (Junkun/Nigeria).

At the beginning of time, there was only darkness and water, and Bumba, the creator, the first ancestor, was alone. Then he vomited up the sun, and there was light. The water dried up, and the outlines of landforms began to emerge. Bumba vomited up the moon and stars. Then he vomited again, and a leopard emerged, then a crested eagle, a crocodile, a fish, a tortoise, and lightning, the heron, a beetle, and a goat. Finally, many men came out. Other animals were then created by those creatures: the heron created birds, the crocodile made serpents and iguana, the goat made horned beasts. The fish created the varieties of fish, the beetle created all other insects. The serpents made grasshoppers, and the iguana made creatures without horns. And the three sons of Bumba finished the world. . . . Bumba then showed the people how to draw fire out of trees, telling them that every tree contained fire. He showed them how to bring fire from the tree. When the creation was complete, Bumba gave these creations to the humans (Bushongo, Democratic Republic of the Congo).

These four stories form only a very small sample. There are hundreds of African stories of creation that have been collected in several books. My favorite is Doondari's story. The aim here is not to reproduce all of them but to attempt to correlate them with our Christian creation-faith in a way that makes sense from the perspective of African Christians.

Like the Bible, African religious expressions do not have a systematically elaborated theology of creation. But by sifting through the vast collection of African creation stories we can paint in very broad strokes some elements of a religious understanding of creation or what I have been referring to as creation-faith. Another common source of such elements is names. Just as many African proper names bear evidence of the belief in the existence of God, as I pointed out in chapter 2, so also do they bear evidence of belief in a supreme creator God. What do African stories tell us about creation?

In general creation is attributed to a *divine being* (or God). This being is completely free to create of itself or, in some cases, *delegate the power to create* to another being(s). In either case, creation is neither partial nor limited; it is always a *cosmic affair*. According to these African stories, nothing falls outside the creating power of the creator God. Hence, the Supreme God remains the ultimate reason and explanation for all things that exist. This recalls some aspects of what was outlined above as the Christian doctrine of creation.

The *mode of creation* varies. Sometimes God calls forth elements of nature into existence; other times the Supreme Being organizes the chaotic elements of nature into a more orderly universe, while at other instances some material is needed to shape and fashion creation. And at still other times, the creating agent simply supervises the process as it is executed by some dependent agents.

A generic term for creation is *life*. Human beings, animals, plants, and objects of nature are all imbued with life. This belief is at the origin of the much-talked-about African *respect for creation*: life as it is present in creation is sacred. Beside the respect accorded to human life on account of its sacredness, African religious expressions advocate reverence for nature. Some animals are considered sacred and may not be killed or eaten for food; some natural elements (rocks, groves, streams, mountains, and so on) are considered sacred because they are the abode of the gods, goddesses, spirits, deities, and ancestors; some plants are revered (sacred trees, shrubs, and so on) and may be used only for medicinal/curative purposes. Based on this awareness of their affinity with the rest of creation or nature, one of the primary concerns of Africans is *harmony with nature*, a balanced relationship with the entire universe. A breach of this harmony can result in nefarious consequences, hence, the constant preoccupation—for which as Africans we are known—with taming, controlling, placating, or neutralizing potentially harmful elements in our relationship with nature.

On the evidence of this brief analysis, we can draw the following conclusions. Creation is primarily a matter of faith: we believe that God created the universe and all that exists in it. Creation depends on God and returns to God. How this happens is a matter of further elaboration and creative imagination, evidence of which we see in the Bible and in many African stories of creation. Finally, for us Africans, creation makes sense from the perspective of the Christian affirmation that in God we live and move and have our being.

Questions for Reflection and Group Discussion

1. Reread the four African stories of creation told in this chapter: What similarities and differences exist between them and the accounts of creation in Genesis?

2. Identify some names in your culture and language that talk about creation by God: what do they say about God's activity in the world and the meaning of creation?

3. According to the stories of creation in Genesis, what should be our attitude toward the created universe and all that it contains?

—〇—

In Praise of the God of Creation

Creation stories abound in African folklore. They tell ancient tales of how the earth and the universe came to be. These tales are a deep wellspring of African creation spiritualities and an inspiration for this prayer in praise of the God of creation.

Ageless One, Creator,
From before before, when only water and darkness
  existed
You formed the earth with a grain of sand.
You created our mothers and fathers from a drop of
  milk.

From your deep womb came fire to light sun, moon,
  stars.
You raised mountains high, moulded hills round, dug
  valleys deep.
You stretched rivers long, filled lakes to the brim,
  spread oceans wide.
You caused thunder to rumble, lightning to flash, rain
  to fall.
You planted green fields, thick bushes, mighty forests.
You fixed wings on birds, fins on fishes, limbs to
  animals.

From the same bowl you ate *ugali* and *fufu*, and drank
  palm-wine with our ancestors.

You taught them to grow crops, melt iron, harvest salt,
    grind grains
Until our greed and selfishness caused you to retreat
    into your great sky hut
And there was death.

Still, from your great sky hut you lower your ageless
    umbilical cord.
You draw us back into your deep womb of love and
    compassion, to live a thousand thousand moons
    with our ancestors.
That is why we raise our voices and sing of the wonder
    of your creation, the grandeur of your wisdom. . . .

Peace Prayer: Africa

Africa continues to be beset by conflicts of monumental proportions; it is a continent thirsty for peace, harmony, and reconciliation. The grandeur and immensity of some of Africa's natural landmarks serve as the inspiration for this community evocation of peace on the continent.

From the shimmering peak of Kilimanjaro,
Response: Let peace be upon Africa!
From the unreachable depth of Lakes Nyasa,
    Tanganyika, Tchad, and Turkana,
Response: Let peace be upon Africa!
From the ancient pyramids of Egypt,
Response: Let peace be upon Africa!
From the meandering rivers of the Nile, Zambezi,
    Congo, Niger, and Limpopo,
Response: Let peace be upon Africa!
From the mighty cascades of Victoria Falls,
Response: Let peace be upon Africa!

From the rolling dunes of the Sahara,
Response: Let peace be upon Africa!
From the sandy plains of the Kalahari,
Response: Let peace be upon Africa!
From the belching volcanoes of the Great Lakes Region,
Response: Let peace be upon Africa!
From the gaping gorges of the Rift Valley,
Response: Let peace be upon Africa!
From the mighty forest of Ituri,
Response: Let peace be upon Africa!

5

Mama Mercy Meets Lady Grace

The story is told of a devout African Christian who implored God in a particularly fervent manner as follows: "Dear God, have *mercy* and give me *grace*! Have *mercy* and give me *grace*!" His wife, who happened to be eavesdropping on her husband's passionate plea for *grace*, was both perplexed and infuriated. Her name was Mercy. So who was this other woman, "Grace," whom he would rather have God give him in place of her? she wondered, as she interrupted her husband's prayer of supplication to interrogate him on the serious matter of his marital infidelity.

This chapter deals with grace, not to be confused with the Grace with whom Mama Mercy thought her husband was having an affair. The following quotations will help set the context for our reflection on the meaning and experience of grace:

> Indeed we also work, but we are only collaborating with God who works, for God's mercy has gone before us. It has gone before us so that we may be healed, and follows us so that once healed, we may be given life; it goes before us so that we may be called, and follows us so that we may be glorified; it goes before us so that we may live devoutly, and follows us so that we may live always with God: for without God we can do nothing. (St. Augustine [354-430])

> From the very beginning the word grace in the Christian vocabulary has stood for the favor and love that God bestows upon humanity in Christ. . . . The word empha-

sizes the qualities of that love of God for human beings; it is totally gratuitous, offered to us in complete freedom on God's part. (Roger Haight, *The Experience and Language of Grace* [Mahwah, N.J.: Paulist Press, 1979] 248)

These quotes talk about a common Christian experience, which theology refers to as "grace." How does the word grace translate in your language? During my preparation for reception into the Catholic Church, the catechist defined grace as the *supernatural gift* of God given to us for the sanctification of our souls. At the time I knew Grace was a common name for a woman, but I had no idea how "she" could be "supernatural" and "sanctify" my soul. Now I know that each one of the terms that make up this definition is loaded with meaning. Grace means a favor that God freely gives to us; it is meant to help us in our journey of faith. Another way of saying this is that grace comes from God as unmerited gift; it empowers us to respond to God's invitation to God's offer of love. Ultimately, grace helps us to live our lives as we were originally meant to live them: as women and men created in the image and likeness of God in whom lie our origin, purpose, and destiny.

In the preceding chapter we spent time reflecting on the doctrine and experience of creation. We can talk about creation because God willed and loved all things that exist into life—from "nothing" to existence. This implies that God's will, love, and life preceded creation itself. Therefore, God's love is not an afterthought. Similarly, the praise and worship that creation renders to God are possible only because God has created all things, and us in particular, with the gift or power to make a free response. We are created to be friends of God, as Abraham was (2 Chron 20:7) and sharers of God's companionship in the cool of the evening breeze (Gen 3:8). This response is possible only with the help of God, which precedes, generates, and enables it. Christian theology calls this help "grace." In my language, Benin, it translates as *esohe*—"unmerited abundant gift."

The story of Okonkwo's first son, Nwoye, illustrates the experience of grace as an offer of a relationship that enables and invites a response: "Although Nwoye had been attracted to the new faith from the very first day, he kept it secret. He dared not go too near the missionaries for fear of his father. But whenever they came to preach in the open marketplace or the village playground, Nwoye was there. And he was already beginning to know some of the simple stories they told." Later on, he would actually take the plunge and embrace the new faith. Grace is *call and response.*

To the acclamation "God is good" many African Christians are used to responding with a resounding "All the time!" The Bible goes further and tells us, "The LORD is gracious and merciful, slow to anger and abounding in steadfast love" (Ps 145:8). The New Testament makes the equation even simpler, more explicit, and profound: God is love (1 John 4:8, 16). This *love is relational.* God is good to us; God is love for us, and God loves us. Another name for this love is grace, not the same as the one Mama Mercy confused with her husband's mystery lover. Like love, *grace is relational.*

To say that grace is relational implies thinking of it less as a thing, which we either possess or do not possess, and more as God's permanent, loving relationship, which is always on offer, a gift to which we are invited to make a free and equally loving response. Therefore, we can describe grace as shorthand for how God relates to us. God relates to us in love: to forgive and to save us. The whole Bible, particularly the New Testament, bears witness to this truth. In fact, we can say that grace represents the fundamental message of the Bible, from creation through the life, passion, death, and resurrection of Jesus Christ, to Pentecost.

God's divine purpose is to bring us to eternal life through love (see John 3:16). This love has taken flesh and pitched tent in our midst (John 1:14), and this love is Jesus Christ, who comes to bring us to the fullness of God's life (John 10:10). No matter how we choose to describe it, God's love brings us salvation. Therefore, *grace is salvation.* It is God's personal self-communication to us, which has no other purpose than to invite us into the fullness of God's own life. In other words, grace is God *as God for us, God at work for us, God in love with us through Christ, in the Spirit.* With so great a love on our side, what can we not do? This love empowers us to be just what God made us to be—sons and daughters of God (John 1:12; 1 John 3:1; Rom 8:14, 16).

When we talk of grace we do so with the understanding that both the initiative and the gift belong to God. And if we can talk about God's love, which is alive and active in us, it is because God has freely and completely bestowed it on us. God takes the initiative; it does not depend on us—it is free! Gratuitous and unmerited, these are the key qualities of grace. As St. Augustine once said, if grace were devoid of these qualities, "Grace would no longer be grace."

God's free offer, favor, and unmerited help are given to us where we are: here and now, in the ordinary events and circumstances of our life. It is also in these ordinary events and circumstances that we respond to God's offer.

Amazing Grace

A popular classic of Christian hymnody is "Amazing Grace":

> Amazing grace! How sweet the sound
> That saved a wretch like me!
> I once was lost, but now am found
> Was blind, but now I see.

It is not easy to talk about the effects of grace. If, as I have said, grace is shorthand for God's self-giving, self-communication, and loving relationship to and with us, it becomes impossible and pretentious to circumscribe the effects of this relationship in our lives. The possibilities are endless. There is no limit to what God's grace can effect in our lives. Nevertheless, it is helpful to highlight certain points or areas of emphasis.

Paul writes to the Romans: "Where sin increased, grace abounded all the more" (5:20). One of the immediate effects of a positive response to the offer of a personal relationship with Jesus Christ comes in the form of the experience of liberation. One might ask: Liberation from what? Liberation for what? We can give a short answer: liberation from sin, and the temptation that holds us captive to sin. In a certain sense we can talk of what John the Evangelist refers to as the "sin of the world" (John 1:29), that pervasive pall of evil that hangs over our world and manifests itself in so many different guises (injustice, oppression, discrimination, violence, marginalization, poverty, idolatry, and so on), and whose effects we all are exposed to. It precedes us; oftentimes we participate in and also help to perpetuate it. But God's offer of forgiveness is universal, always seeking to overcome evil and our resistance and excuses. Sin continues to hold us captive to the extent that we resist the grace of God, but it does not diminish God's love for us. God says as much in the prophecy of Isaiah: "Even if these may forget, yet I will not forget you" (49:15). God loves us by name and by face, as unique individuals. To the question I asked above, "For what does grace free us?" we can respond quite simply: Grace empowers us to respond freely and lovingly to God's invitation to love.

Paul writes, moreover, to the Galatians: "For freedom Christ has set us free. Stand firm, therefore, and do not submit again to a yoke of slavery" (5:1). This freedom has a special character. It is not a license "to do and undo." Nor is it merely a freedom *from* the power of sin. We are freed *for* something: we are freed for love. God's grace gives us the strength we need to reach beyond ourselves, so that we can love *in the direction of God*. Our self-centeredness and selfishness may impose limits; grace helps us to transcend those obstacles to love. Freedom to love is impossible without God's help or grace.

God acts within freedom, never against it. God's grace does not compel or coerce us. Otherwise, to repeat what St. Augustine said, grace would no longer be grace. Freedom is not passive either; God empowers it to take initiatives for love. Thus, this initiative, impetus, or impulse to love does not compete with or stifle our freedom as human beings. Grace neither competes with nor destroys nature. Sin is what competes with grace. The aim of grace, therefore, is to stimulate cooperation with what God is doing in our lives. Grace, which helps us to choose life, never destroys our freedom to make that choice and our free response.

As mentioned above, a few days later, Nwoye would make the decisive move to respond to the invitation that had been stirring in his young mind since his very first encounter with the Christian missionaries. After a particularly violent reaction from his father,

Nwoye "went back to the church and told Mr. Kiaga that he had decided to go to Umuofia where the white missionary had set up a school to teach young Christians to read and write." His journey of faith as a Christian had begun—*by the grace of God*.

The very nature of Jesus' proclamation suggests that God invites us to share or participate in God's life. That, as we will recall, is also the purpose of creation—to walk in the cool of the evening breeze with God. Christian theology speaks about grace as having a deifying, *divinizing,* or sanctifying effect. Because God's love is made flesh in our lives, our own lives can now take on the qualities of God's own life. God's favor and love re-create and re-constitute us in God's own image, transforming us into what the psalmist describes as just "a little lower than God" and "crowned with glory and honor" (Ps 8:5). To this Jesus would add: "Be perfect, as your God is perfect" (Matt 5:48).

A Serious Offense

"What is sin?" asked the catechist. "A serious offense against God," replied the catechumen. Simple, short, and precise.

We have seen that grace—as an experience of God's unconditional love—precedes us. We are born into grace, which is always on offer. But then, there is the reality of sin, to which I alluded in the preceding section. This reality has been the subject of many heated debates, as theologians and philosophers struggle to come to an understanding of sin and what it means in the lives of Christians. It has been defined, classified, and categorized in many different ways. One thing we need to bear in mind is that sin is not merely the subject of an abstract theological discourse. Sin has a face and a name; it is an experience we all are caught up in. It is the thorn in the flesh of our human condition.

In the next few paragraphs, I will focus the reflection on the pervasive *nature or reality* of sin, and less on sinful *acts*. In my catechism class, one of the ways in which we identified sin was to list the Ten Commandments: "Thou shalt not. . . ." In that way we knew the dos and don'ts of Christianity. There were no excuses.

The catechist also told us about "original sin." As a teenage catechumen the only meaning I could associate with "original" was "real and authentic," as opposed to "fake and counterfeit." So the question that agitated my young Catholic mind was: What does an *original* sin or a *fake* sin look like?

The meaning of this category—what I prefer to call a theological symbol—known as original sin has been hotly debated and has come to mean many different things in our understanding of the condition of human existence. Some would argue that it is original because it takes place at the dawn of creation and is also the reason for which we have become implicated in the history of sin. The consequence of this sin is what Genesis describes as the Fall. This foundational reality has left its imprint on the condition of human existence. Perhaps it is more accurate to see sin as coming to existence at the dawn of human freedom and responsibility. This is what the story of Adam and Eve in the garden of creation tries to tell us in the contemporary language of its writer(s).

The primary source of the Christian doctrine of sin is Genesis 3. Many African creation stories recount a similar pattern of events that lead to sin or a split in the once harmonious relationship between the creator and his or her creatures. A good example is the story of Kiumbi, recounted in chapter 4. In that story, as in other similar African accounts of creation, God withdraws or retreats to a remote abode, usually above, in the heavens. This is unlike the Genesis account, in which God expels Adam and Eve from Eden.

According to the Genesis account, after the creation of the world, God commands Adam and Eve to steer clear of the fruit of a certain tree. The temptation is too much for the first parents, and they eventually succumb. Consequently, everything begins to go wrong. The harmonious condition of human existence, which God had taken so much pride in only "a few days" earlier, is completely ruptured. Adam and Eve are estranged from each other and from the rest of creation. Worse still, they are both alienated from the harmonious bliss that once characterized their relationship with God. In popular parlance, we might call this a complete fall "from grace to grass!"

We also see Paul reflecting seriously on the pervasiveness and

tenacity of sin's grip on human existence (Rom 7:14-25). So strong
are the power and the force that he even personifies them. This
force of sin is operative in human existence, and it exercises a limit-
ing influence on human freedom to believe, to love, and to hope.
Yet, the key point that we often forget is that God's love precedes
this state of human sinfulness, and this same love alone holds the
key to redemption from the negative consequences of sin. Paul
appears to have understood this: "Wretched man that I am! Who
will rescue me from this body of death? Thanks be to God through
Jesus Christ our Lord!" declares Paul in Romans 7:24-25.

What needs to be retained as essential in the understanding
of sin is the universality of grace. Christ is our savior, the savior of
all who have sinned. In Catholic theology this belief was so radically safeguarded that it even made provision for infants who were
thought to have inherited original sin from their parents—just
in case they died before receiving the grace of baptism! This is a
somewhat extreme position; it dates back to the teachings of St.
Augustine, who was reacting to a group of Christians called the
Pelagians. They had a more optimistic approach to the capacity of
human will to effect salvation on its own, something that Augustine found erroneous.

What does the account of original sin in Genesis 3 really tell
us? The Bible does not call it original sin. That is a later invention.
First, it is important to see it as a *symbolic* account. Therefore, it has
a message that goes deeper than the text or the story itself. We can
summarize this message as follows: Because of the abuse or less-
than-adequate use of our God-given freedom, we are not what or
who God really intends us to be; we are drawn toward sin; no one
is spared this propensity or inclination to sin; we constantly look
for excuses and alibis for our less-than-human acts or responses to
God's loving and life-giving invitation.

Furthermore, Genesis 3 hints at the fact that sin exists before
us, in the sense that it is "something" we discover subsequent to
the exercise of human freedom. It is in this *human freedom* that it
locates the origin of sin, not in God. God creates what is good; as
humans we choose what is less than good. Considered from the
perspective of the exercise of human freedom, sin becomes an abuse

or misuse of human freedom. Thus, Genesis 3 tells us a lot about how sin operates in our lives *today*, rather than how the serpent tricked Eve and she in turn persuaded the unsuspecting Adam to eat the "forbidden fruit."

In short, the story of Eve and Adam tells us that human freedom can and does rebel against God, against love. It has happened before, it still happens today, and it will continue to happen among individuals, societies, and nations. The implication of this assertion is that, without exception, we all stand in need of the universal saving and liberating grace offered by Jesus Christ.

So far we have established that sin is not merely an abstract concept; it is an existential reality. We cannot define the condition of human existence without it, just as human existence makes no sense without grace. This grace is God's love and self-communication in Christ, which is always on offer. Do we respond positively to it or resist it? The result, depending on the choice we make, is called grace or sin, freedom or slavery. Thus, we cannot define sin apart from freedom; it is the means by which we actualize sin. God respects our freedom. Without this respect, we cannot be human beings created free—even though God knows freedom includes the possibility of rejecting God. This possibility is not sin; actualizing it is sin. We cannot define sin apart from grace either. Grace offers the efficacious possibility or means for overcoming the grip of sin on human existence.

A Communal and Cosmic Affair

Tanzanian theologian Laurenti Magesa writes as follows in his book *African Religion: The Moral Traditions of Abundant Life*:

> In African Religion, wrongdoing relates to the contravention of specific codes of community expectations, including taboos. Individuals and the whole community must observe these forms of behavior to preserve order and assure the continuation of life in its fullness. To threaten

in any way to break any of the community codes of behavior, which are in fact moral codes, endangers life; it is bad, wrong or "sinful." (p. 166)

We can begin with the presupposition that the way sin is generally understood in African religious expressions can enrich the Christian doctrine of sin. As we have seen, this latter draws on certain biblical sources and lays heavy emphasis on the role of the *individual's* freedom in actualizing the possibility of sin. As a religious concept and human experience, sin is not alien to African religious expressions. The conception may be compared to the Western/Christian understanding, because it includes the essential reality of a break, a rupture, and a loss of harmony. There is a fundamental difference, however: If sin is an offense against God, as my catechist taught me (what we might designate as the vertical axis), as an African I am more inclined to consider it as a disruption of the harmony between the composite parts or elements of the universe (which we might call the horizontal axis).

In the chapter on creation I pointed out the preoccupation of Africans with harmony—cosmic harmony between and among humans, animals, vegetation, and all the elements of nature. Many African stories of creation also give an account of the origin of sin in the world. This cosmic understanding of sin in Africa means that its effects are more rather than less destructive. Besides, it also implies that sin is not a neutral reality: it has consequences both for the doer and for the rest of the community. In the *Zairean Rite for the Celebration of the Eucharistic Liturgy,* sin and evil are likened to "the insect that sticks on to our skin and sucks our blood." When we recall that life is a shared reality and event in Africa, it makes sense to think of sin as the poisoning of the community's life blood. That was precisely how the people of Umuofia understood the gravity of Okonkwo's violation of an important religious code. As the story goes, Okonkwo beat his youngest wife in a fit of rage during the Week of Peace. The laws of the land forbade such acts of violence, and Ezeani, the chief priest of the earth goddess, in no uncertain terms reminded Okonkwo of the consequences of his action:

"Listen to me," he said when Okonkwo had spoken. "You are not a stranger in Umuofia. You know as well as I do that our forefathers ordained that before we plant any crops in the earth we should observe a week in which a man does not say a harsh word to his neighbor. We live in peace with our fellows to honor our great goddess of the earth without whose blessing our crops will not grow. You have committed a great evil. . . ."

The experience of sin can be understood within the much wider context of life. According to African religious expressions, life stands for a wide concept; it embraces the world of the yet-to-be-born, the living, the living dead (ancestors), and all other categories of animal and plant life, as well as the world of nature. Life constitutes the most basic category of the African's religious worldview, and sin is, as Magesa points out, anything that diminishes, opposes, or destroys this life. Since life is a shared category rather than isolated in the individual, it is within the larger communal experience that sin makes the most sense. Magesa, for example, treats sin under the general title of "enemies of life." This shows clearly the kind of context within which the African experiences and comprehends the reality of sin or wrongdoing.

On the basis of the above reflection, we perceive more clearly the fact that sin is not a reality to be dealt with solely on the level of abstraction; it manifests itself as concrete and experiential and has palpable effects on the destiny of the individual in community. There is always an agent (human or spiritual) behind or at the origin of the evil or sinful act, and this act exists as such only in the actions of people toward one another. In other words, *sin is relational*. Something is considered as sinful insofar as it destroys the life of the doer and the life that he or she shares with the rest of the community and nature. Ezeani's greatest concern was the potential consequences of Okonkwo's action for the entire clan. In his own words, "The evil you have done can ruin the whole clan. The earth goddess whom you have insulted may refuse to give us her increase, and we shall all perish."

In the same vein certain African religious expressions locate the origin of sin in certain parts of the human anatomy, such as the head, the heart, the stomach, and the eye. It is believed that there can be a particular concentration of evil in these parts. In other words, these parts are the seat of harmful intentions (see Matt 12:34; 6:22-23; 15:10-20). These intentions are translated from these organs into acts that are detrimental to life. It is common to find the following expressions in African languages: "bad heart," "dirty stomach," "bad head," and "evil eye."

African religious expressions emphasize avoiding wrongdoing or sin but place an even greater importance on consciously pursuing acts that enhance the general state of life of the community and maintain the general state of harmony between all participants in the reality called life. To the extent that this happens we can also talk of grace in action. Conversely, to the extent that it is impeded, we can talk of the evil of sin.

To conclude this chapter, a brief word on reconciliation and forgiveness is in order. In general, the way Africans understand sin also determines to a large extent their understanding of forgiveness and reconciliation. Reconciliation involves a process, of which a personal interior feeling of remorse and guilt is only one stage. The other stages include a public confession, that is, in the presence of the community or extended (or more immediate) family, a punishment (usually a fine), a ritual cleansing, and reconciliation proper. After reprimanding Okonkwo for violating the Week of Peace, the priest of the earth goddesses imposed a fine: "His tone now changed from anger to command. 'You will bring to the shrine of Ani tomorrow one she-goat, one hen, a length of cloth and a hundred cowries.' He rose and left the hut."

As an African proverb says, if one finger brings oil, it soils all the others. To which we can add: if one finger is cleaned, all the others also become clean. The ultimate grace of reconciliation is the restoration of the original harmony with God, self, community, and nature.

From the perspective of the foregoing, God's grace appears as more than just a help toward virtuous acts; it embodies the very possibility of redemption for individuals as well as for the community and the entire universe. If sin has universal consequences, grace embodies a cosmic gift offered to us for the redemption of our world.

Questions for Reflection and Group Discussion

1. How would you translate "grace" in your mother tongue? What does it mean?

2. How would you translate "sin" in your mother tongue? What does it mean? Does it mean the same thing for individuals and for the family or community?

3. How is reconciliation carried out in your culture? Is there any religious ritual of reconciliation? What are the various elements or stages of this ritual?

—❦—

An African Prayer of Lamentation in Confidence
Inspired by titles of some novels and books about Africa

God of our Brother, Jesus Christ,

Things are falling apart in Africa, and we are *no longer at ease;* the evils that torment us are like an *open sore.*[1]

Daily we walk upon *the famished road* to parched farmlands *dying in the sun;* our hunt for food is like *striving for the wind;* in vain we search for *a grain of wheat* in our empty granaries.[2]

At sunset we walk *the narrow path* back *to the shadows* of the night; on our bamboo beds we contemplate *fragments* of our broken dreams; we lack even *the will to die.*[3]

---

1. Chinua Achebe; Wole Soyinka.
2. Ben Okri; Peter K. Palangyo; Meja Mwangi; James Ngugi.
3. Francis Selormey; Robert Serumaga; Ayi Kwei Armah; Can Themba.

God of our Brother, Jesus Christ,

Hear *the voice* of Africa; heal *the wound* and *tribal scars*
that have disfigured the face of our continent; lead
us with compassion on our *long walk to freedom.*[4]

Free us from the evil that keeps us *bound to violence;*
may our children live more than *a few nights and
days.*[5]

When our eyes are shut in death, may we never
become a *carcass for hounds;* bring us in safety *into
the house of the ancestors;* where we may dwell in
peace for *two thousand seasons.*[6]

Amen.

---

4. Gabriel Okara; Malick Fall; Sembene Ousmane; Nelson Mandela.
5. Yembo Oulogeme; Mbella Sonne Dipoko.
6. Meja Mwangi; Karl Maier; Ayi Kwei Armah.

6

I Said "God Had a Son," But I Did Not Say "He Had a Wife"!

In chapter 3 we saw the interesting story of the missionary in the village of Mbanta who tried to explain to the skeptical villagers how God came to have a son called *Jesu Kristi* without first having a wife. The missionary failed woefully to impress his prospective converts with his explanation. But he was not the first to ask about or try to explain the identity and personality of Jesus Christ. Jesus himself was curious to know what people thought of him:

> Now when Jesus went into the district of Caesarea Philippi, he asked his disciples, "Who do people say that the Son of Man is?" And they said, "Some say John the Baptist, but others Elijah, and still others Jeremiah or one of the prophets." He said to them, "But who do you say that I am?" Simon Peter answered, "You are the Messiah, the Son of the living God." (Matt 16:13-16)

In this story from the Gospel of Matthew Jesus posed what we might call in popular parlance the million-dollar question: Who am I? Over the centuries, Christians in general and theologians in particular have grappled with the same question. Today, if we put the question randomly to a group of Christians, or even to passersby, their responses, though varied, would be essentially similar to that of Jesus' disciples: Son of God, my savior, my Lord, miracle worker, king of kings, my greatest friend, good shepherd, universal lover, the second person of the Blessed Trinity, and so on. Each man or woman who bears the title Christian will definitely have a response to the question.

The particular branch of theology that deals with this question is known as Christology, that is, the theological study of Jesus Christ. As Christians, we recognize Jesus Christ as the center of our Christian faith; we profess our belief in God, in and through Jesus Christ: "I believe in Jesus Christ, the only Son of God." Our word about God (or theology) would be seriously deficient if it ignored Christology, that is, our word about Christ.

In theology there are many ways of approaching the question of Jesus Christ. One could choose to consider it from the perspective of classical theological controversies. Around the fourth century c.e., for example, heated debates erupted in the church concerning the divinity of Christ, on the one hand, and the completeness (or even genuineness) of his humanity, on the other. Another way of approaching the question could be from the point of view of the so-called Jesus debate, that is, the quest for the historical Jesus: Who was *the man* that lived and died in Palestine a little over two thousand years ago? What did he *actually say and do*? What were the cultural, historical, socio-economic, and political circumstances of *his life and times*? Here we would be looking for the material evidence that this first-century Palestinian who is the central figure of the New Testament actually existed. Hollywood movies, such as *Jesus Christ Superstar, The Last Temptation of Jesus Christ,* and bestsellers, such as *The Last Temptation of Christ* and *The Da Vinci Code,* represent contemporary, albeit fantastical, representations of the Jesus debate. We could also tackle the question of Jesus Christ from the angle of what some theologians call "the Jesus of faith," that is, Jesus Christ the Lord, as the early Christian communities understood and interpreted *theologically* the events of his life, passion, death, and resurrection, and the universal significance of Christ for our world today.

For the last of these three approaches, the primary sources will be the four Gospels (Mathew, Mark, Luke, and John). These Gospels do not *primarily* tell a history; they tell *his*-story. Their primary purpose is not history for the sake of recounting and relating concrete and objective data and facts. The primary purpose is faith. As the writer in John put it so beautifully, "Now Jesus did many other signs in the presence of his disciples, which are not written in this book. But these are written that you may come to believe that Jesus is the Messiah, the Son of God, and that through believing you may have life in his name" (20:30-31). The evangelist's purpose is unambiguous: faith not facts. So, let us talk about *Jesu Kristi* from the point of view of our faith.

From the evidence of the Gospels, Jesus' life unfolded as a whole: he was born, he lived, taught, and worked among his people. Then he got into serious trouble with the religious and political authorities; he was condemned, put to death, and rose again three days later. During his lifetime the meaning and purpose of Jesus' life and work were variously perceived and interpreted depending on the audience. His birth generated both anxiety and eager anticipation: "Where is the child who has been born king of the Jews?" (Matt 2:2). "Are you the one who is to come, or are we to wait for another?" (Matt 11:3). For some people he was an awe-inspiring preacher, whose words commanded the obedience of both natural and supernatural forces (Matt 7:28-29; 8:27; 12:22-23). He had a somewhat strained relationship with his immediate family (Mark 3:20-21; 6:1-6). His teaching, public pronouncements, and ministry drew the ire of his adversaries (Mark 3:6; Luke 4:28-30; John 8:59; 11:45-53). He had his own convictions about his relationship with God, whom he affectionately called *Abba* (Matt 11:25-27; John 5:19-47; 14:6-14), and the mission entrusted to him (Luke 4:16-21; Mark 1:15; 10:45). Oftentimes, things did not go well between him and his adversaries. Eventually, things came to a head. He was betrayed, tried, condemned, put to death, and was buried, *"but on the third day he rose again in fulfillment of the Scriptures"*—as Christians profess in the creed.

The raising of Jesus Christ from the dead became the kernel of the good news (gospel), which the apostles felt duty bound to proclaim to "the end of the age":

> For I handed on to you as of first importance what I in turn had received: that Christ died for our sins in accordance with the scriptures, and that he was buried, and

that he was raised on the third day in accordance with the
scriptures. (1 Cor 15:3-5)

From this astonishing experience emerged what theologians
now call "resurrection faith," that is, belief in Jesus Christ, Son of
God, and savior of the world.

The purpose of the above summary is to emphasize the point
that what we have in the four Gospels is already a theological interpretation of the *enduring meaning and universal significance* of Jesus
Christ. Behind each Gospel there is a community (as well as a
writer, an editor, or redactor). For each of these communities Jesus
had a unique significance. Thus, as John tells us very plainly, the
Gospels were written as a testament of the faith of a believing community (1 John 1:1-5). In other words, they are written from faith,
in faith, with faith, for faith, and by faith. So, we can talk about the
Jesus of Matthew, Mark, Luke, and John.

The way in which each of these faith communities understood
Jesus was very unique. Nevertheless, we can still identify some
major points of convergence on the life, mission, teaching, death,
and resurrection of Jesus the Lord. In other words, each of the four
Gospels has a kernel of how the respective early communities experienced and understood Jesus. This kernel is what forms the gospel
message, such as the one proclaimed by Paul (1 Cor 15:3-5). Each
of the early communities had its own Christology or Christologies.
One way of coming to a clearer understanding of this Christology
is to look at the titles attributed to Jesus in the four Gospels. The
list is a fairly long one: Son of God, Lord, Teacher, Rabbi, Messiah,
Savior of the World, Prophet, King of Israel, Judge, Friend, Son of
Joseph the carpenter, Good Shepherd, Son of David, I Am, Son of
Man, and so on. These christological labels or titles do not tell the
whole story about Jesus, but they do reveal something of how the
early communities understood and interpreted the significance of
his person and mission. In light of modern advances in theological
and scriptural research, these interpretations should be treated as
such: they are partial rather than absolute theological statements
or exclusive biblical interpretations that attempt to answer the
question "Who do you say that I am?"

"Messiah Is the King of Kings,
Messiah Is the Lord of Lords"
(A Popular African Song)

In a short book such as this one, it is not possible to examine all the titles and names attributed to Jesus in the four Gospels. Many books have been written and continue to be written about them. By way of example, let us consider just one of them to get a taste of the richness and depth of these titles. We shall look at "Messiah." It is important to understand that this term is a Hebrew scriptural symbol, which gives us a way of understanding Jesus.

If we take a look at Mark's Gospel we encounter Jesus the Messiah and Son of God at the very beginning of his Gospel (1:1). Not so in the Gospel of John. Here we encounter these titles at the end, as if John intended them as some kind of a summary of the content of faith that he wished to proclaim and confirm (20:31). Scholars believe that the title "Messiah" has its origin at the heart of the Jewish tradition that anticipated the deliverance of the people from the political and economic oppression that they faced. We can only understand its meaning when we situate it within the context of the long and beleaguered religious tradition and history of the Jews as told in the Bible.

When the messianic titles occur in John, they appear within the context or framework of contemporary Judaism. Who is the Messiah? He is the one whom God has anointed and commissioned to assist God in the (re)establishment of God's dominion at the end of time. For John, it looks back to a glory achieved and a prophecy fulfilled. It embodies the people's ongoing aspirations and resilient hope for the restoration of the lost Kingdom of Judah. It is not surprising, therefore, that when John introduces these messianic titles the ultimate intention is to vindicate the claims associated with them. It is a controversial attempt to marry the hope of "contemporary" Jews with the significance of Jesus' mission, as perceived by John and his community. This attempt shows up in many confrontations between Jesus and his listeners. It is present, for example, in the encounter with the Samaritan woman (chap. 4), Peter's confession (6:69), the great debate with the Pharisees (chap. 7), the occasion for the expulsion of the man born blind (chap. 9), Martha's confession (11:27), and the purpose of the Gospel (20:31).

With the exception of chapters 4 and 7, however, the messianic theme is not really one that fires up the theological imagination and interest of John, certainly much less than does the title "Son of God." In spite of the frequent occurrence of "Messiah," John uses it mostly as part of a proper name: Jesus (the) Christ, "the anointed one." Why is it so? One explanation suggests that it belongs to a very early stage of the composition of this Gospel. At that stage, perhaps, the community of John, the Johannine Christians, was still part and parcel of the local synagogue community. Their only mark of distinction could have been that they believed that Andrew's words "We have found the Messiah" (1:41) contained some truth. This early stage of the writing of the Gospel of John—focusing on the affirmation of Jesus' messianic status—will gradually become less and less relevant as the community graduates to a much "higher" Christology, such as one based on the titles Son of God and Son of Man.

If we consider, for example, John 1:19-51, we see a certain trajectory of how faith in the messianic identity of Jesus progresses to a discovery and affirmation of his status, first as Son of God, and, ultimately, as Son of Man. Toward the end of this passage, Nathaniel makes the triumphant declaration: "You are the Son of God! You are the King of Israel!" (v. 49). But his assertion is only a penultimate proclamation of the true identity of Jesus. The ultimate identity of Jesus is revealed by Jesus himself: "Very truly, I tell you, you will see heaven opened and the angels of God ascending and descending upon the Son of Man" (v. 51). With this revelation the cycle of discovery and confession of who Jesus truly is for the community of John reaches its climax. Not simply Messiah ("about whom Moses in the law and also the prophets wrote" [v. 45]), not just Son of God (God's special envoy who shares in the authority and divinity of God [10:30, 10:38; 14:2, 14:10]), but Son of Man (the exalted and glorified judge, the sole mediator between heaven and earth [3:14; 8:28; 12:23, 34; 13:31]).

The point of the foregoing is to show how fascinating the study of the titles of Jesus can be. They are a rich source of the theology of the identity and significance of Jesus Christ, not only for the communities that first used these titles in the four Gospels but also for us today who depend on their testimony and understanding to work out our own answer to the fundamental question of Jesus: "Who do you say that I am?"

Who Are You for Us, Jesu Kristi?

The name *Jesu Kristi* is relatively new in Africa. Africans did not call upon this name before the advent of the Christian missionaries. Nevertheless, *Jesu Kristi* has gained popularity on the lips of African Christians. In many parts of Africa, songs have been written, liturgies composed, and humorous stories told about Jesus in local languages. This popularity embodies a profound quest, namely, the quest for the true face of Jesus. I use the words "true face" deliberately. I wish to show that the Africans' quest for "who Jesus is for us" cannot be satiated by simply adopting christological formulas and models developed in foreign cultural contexts. Some people might object: "It doesn't matter. Jesus transcends culture!" Not quite. Jesus subsumes culture! These are two different understandings.

How can we recast the alien and expatriate images of Jesus Christ in the mold of the rich and colorful African religious and cultural worldview in order to discover an authentic and meaningful African identity and personality of Jesus? This question is not academic; it represents an ongoing search for a *Jesu Kristi* who will be able to respond to questions posed by Africans themselves.

Somewhere in Nigeria there is a church leader who claims to be "Jesus of Oyingbo"! In Kenya, Elijah Masinde of *Dini ya Msambwa* and Ondeto Messiah of *Legio Maria* both declared themselves "the Messiah." Apparently, Ondeto's followers delayed his burial in the hope of his resurrection on the third day. All of them represent the extreme or pathological end of the spectrum of this African christological quest.

So far, the result of this quest, at least in the African theological circle, is a striking litany of christological titles, models, and proposals, along with an extensive job description for the African Christ. We have, for example, the following models or proposals: ancestor, diviner, traditional healer, healer, chief, guest, warrior, life giver, family member, initiator, mediator, intermediary, friend, loved one, brother, elder brother, ideal brother, universal brother, proto-elder, kin, kinsman, chief priest, chief elder, ruler, king, leader, liberator, black messiah, and so on.

Sometimes the plethora of African christological titles and proposals appear to be in conflict with one another. This conflict is more apparent than real. We can discern some elements of convergence among the names and titles depending on the point of departure. Tanzanian theologian Charles Nyamiti, who has written extensively on African Christology, makes this point quite clearly. According to him, some theologians begin from what the Bible says about Jesus Christ and then try to find names and titles in African culture that match the biblical teaching. The second group takes the reverse route. They begin from African culture and work their way toward a meeting point with what the Bible says about the personality and identity of Jesus Christ. Guinean theologian Cécé Kolié offers a good example of the first kind. For him, Jesus is Healer. Before presenting Jesus as Healer, he undertakes a descriptive survey of healing as the principal activity of Jesus in the Gospels, ranging from "specific cures" (for example, exorcisms) to "catechetical cures, resurrections, and social integration." At a second stage, he examines the complex phenomenon of sickness and healing in Africa. His conclusion is an attempt to create a place for Jesus as Healer in Africa, a model that will incorporate both the biblical and the African conception and experience of healing. Congolese theologian François Kabasélé's proposal, Christ-as-Chief, provides a good illustration of the second approach. He begins by identifying and describing the traditional images and symbols of Bantu chiefs and, then, applies these images and symbols to Christ of the Gospels.

Why is Christology so important in Africa? According to Nigerian theologian Enyi B. Udoh, if there is a problem of faith in Africa, that problem derives from the way we understand or misunderstand Jesus Christ. In other words, it is a christological problem. And what is this problem? It has to do with how we can reconcile the relatively new personality of Jesus with what Africans have known and lived as their way to God long before the advent of missionary Christianity. Sometimes the tension created by this problem is such that many African Christians straddle two seemingly opposing worlds. Like the proverbial hyena split in two by indecision, they are neither here nor there. This tension has serious implications for how Africans live their faith in *Jesu Kristi*. While it is convenient for some Africans to profess a nominal adherence to Christianity, in times of socio-economic and cultural distress this superficial profession of Christian faith easily gives way to familiar traditional religious practices, which Christianity claims to have superseded. Jesus Christ seems to disappear from crisis situations in the lives of some African Christians. Desmond Tutu calls this phenomenon "faith schizophrenia." For Udoh, it is "religious double-mindedness." But it is Efoé-Julien Penoukou of Benin who has summed up very well the issue at stake here: "A person who claims to believe in Christ, yet has recourse to other spiritual, cosmic, or metacosmic forces, has not yet succeeded in identifying who Jesus Christ is, that he or she may profess him radically." Why is this so?

I made the point in chapter 2 that Africans are deeply religious people. They were already familiar with the existence and worship of God prior to the advent of Christianity and its claim that Jesus Christ is the sole redeemer of the world. Consequently, the new element that African Christians have to deal with is the figure of Jesus Christ. To quote Robert Hood, "It is not the Christian God who causes problems for Afro cultures; it is the Christian Christ." Zimbabwean theologian Gwinyai Muzorewa once wrote: "Africans knew God, but they did not know God's son, Jesus Christ. As my own father always told me, 'The only new thing the missionaries brought to Africa is Jesus Christ, not God.'" To which Udoh would add: "It is as though the Africans are saying: God we know; ancestors we acknowledge; but who are you for us, Jesus Christ?"

The major task confronting Christology from an African perspective is to develop a clear conception of the person of Jesus Christ and to make Jesus Christ feel at home within the framework or the ordinary experience of African Christians. Contemporary

African christological models are based on categories that their authors claim to be authentically African and speak immediately to the African consciousness. One such category that I shall examine in the next section is Christ as Ancestor.

Jesu Kristi, *Our Ancestor*

The concept of ancestor is familiar to Africans. This does not mean that all Africans form the same concept of ancestor. Divergent conceptions of the meaning and role of ancestors exist among the vast and complex cultural entities of the continent. In spite of these apparent or real divergences, the category of ancestor is authentically African. Some African theologians, like Charles Nyamiti and Bénézet Bujo (Democratic Republic of the Congo), talk about *ancestral Christology*. Let us examine some of the key elements of this model according to these two theologians.

Nyamiti prefers the idea of *brother-ancestor*. A brother-ancestor, as he explains it, shares common parentage with us. To him (or her) belongs the role of mediating between us and God, as well as modeling for us good and proper conduct. In return, we maintain a "sacred communication" with him or her that is not broken by the reality of death.

This definition comprises five essential traits of African ancestorship. First, an ancestor maintains some binding blood ties with the living members of his or her family, clan, or community. In other words, he or she plays a key role in the lives of those with whom he or she maintains such links. As I mentioned above, death does not diminish this role. Second, on the contrary, the experience of death offers the ancestor a privileged place of closeness to God. Consequently, third, he or she is able to mediate or intercede on behalf of the living family or clan members. Fourth, as a result of this role as mediator, he or she is entitled to mandatory and regular communication and consultation (invocation, libation, ritual offerings, sacrifices, and so forth) with the living. And, finally, in order to be raised to the status of the living dead, a person must have distinguished himself or herself in service and led an exemplary life in the community. This is precisely what allows him or her to become a model for the entire family and community of the living.

For Nyamiti, this African brother-ancestorship parallels Christ's ancestorship. Structurally they are the same, because Jesus Christ meets all the prerequisite conditions for the former and, therefore, qualifies to be a brother-ancestor in the African sense of the term. Jesus Christ realizes all that being a brother-ancestor entails: he is mediator and high priest, the archetype of good Christian conduct, to whom is due veneration through sacred communication. But there is a difference. Considering Christ's origin as Son of God, his divine-human personality, and his Trinitarian status (second person of the Trinity), his ancestorship subsumes and eminently transcends the limited notion of brother-ancestorship. Jesus Christ completes and perfects what Africans believe to be brother-ancestor. Christ is no longer one ancestor among many others, but the universal Brother-Ancestor par excellence.

Bujo's understanding of Christ as Ancestor is similar to Nyamiti's. Bujo prefers to call his model "proto-ancestor." For him, the notion of ancestor in Africa is a ritual enactment of the deep-seated belief in the permanence of life, which is guaranteed by the bond that unites the dead and the living. What the African seeks in the cult of the ancestors is not merely a commemoration of the dead, but, more significantly, a *communion* with the living dead.

Taking a retrospective look at the life of Jesus Christ, one discovers that through his mission and ministry he clearly identifies with the saving role of African ancestors. The most important dimension of this role requires that ancestors be the source of life to all the descendants of the living dead. Since Jesus Christ *alone* realizes this ancestral ideal and embodies all its virtues in the "highest degree" by elevating it to a superior level of "new fulfillment," it becomes inadequate to consider Christ merely as one member of the communion of ancestors. As Bujo argues, he is more appropriately to be designated "Proto-Ancestor" or "Proto-Life-Force."

It is obvious that Bujo's and Nyamiti's ancestor models strive to conform to an authentically African mode of thought. There are important similarities in both approaches. In Christ's ancestorship, the mysteries of the Incarnation, death, and resurrection are vital to the actualization of his role as Brother-Ancestor par excellence or as Proto-Ancestor. If the starting point of both theologians appears to be the same, however, their goals differ considerably. Nyamiti builds up an approach that culminates in the formulation of an *ancestral Christology*, while Bujo, taking *ancestral Christology* as a starting point, elaborates a morality of the ancestors (*la morale ancestrale*) that culminates in a "Proto-Ancestor ecclesiology."

Similarly, both authors agree on the role of African ancestors vis-à-vis Jesus Christ. For Nyamiti, in the final analysis, other African ancestors are no more than "poor and faint images" of the Brother-Ancestor, Jesus Christ. Bujo is more careful in his choice of words. For him, the African ancestors are "forerunners" of the Proto-Ancestor. He adapts Hebrews 1:1-2 to explain his idea: "For after God had spoken to us at various times and in various places, including our ancestors, in these last days he speaks to us through his Son, whom he has established as unique Ancestor, as Proto-Ancestor, from whom all life flows for His descendants." Nyamiti and Bujo draw a unanimous conclusion: Jesus Christ is the unique ancestor who completes and perfects all there is in the African conception of ancestor.

"Jesus Is My Bulldozer!"

So, let us return to the question with which we began this chapter: "Who do you say that I am?" A couple of years after my ordination I had the privilege of presiding at the Eucharist in a prison in Benin City, Nigeria. The prison inmates were convinced charismatic Catholics. For the entrance procession they intoned and passionately sang a song that has never ceased to intrigue me:

> Jesus is my bulldozer. Amen! He's my bulldozer, Amen! Bulldoze my case, O Lord! Amen! He's my bulldozer, Amen! Bulldoze the lawyer, O Lord! Amen! He's my bulldozer, Amen! Bulldoze the judge, O Lord! Amen! He's my bulldozer, Amen! Jesus is my bulldozer. Amen! He's my bulldozer, Amen!

Had Jesus addressed the question of Matthew 16 to those Christian convicts of Benin prison, he would have been in for a big surprise. His disciples were much more circumspect. Peter responded with an answer that Jesus affirmed as inspired by God. Peter spoke for himself, based on his experience of faith seeking love and hope. The process he set in motion continues today, as each Christian strives to discover an adequate answer for himself or herself. Unlike Peter, we are not privileged recipients of the revelation that Jesus commended as untainted by "flesh and blood." The theologians presented above offer us an example of their personal quest. Fascinating as theirs might be, neither Nyamiti nor Bujo can claim to speak for all Christians, whether African or not.

Based on his or her flesh-and-blood experience, every African Christian who confesses the God of *Jesu Kristi* faces the challenging task of formulating his or her own answer to the Jesus question. This answer will be conditioned by his or her situation in life and the degree of personal relationship that each one has with *Jesu Kristi*. In other words, the answer will derive from each Christian's personal encounter of *Jesu Kristi*, rather than from the erudite speculations of theologians.

Hence, for the imprisoned Christians of Benin City, only a *Jesu Kristi* endowed with the power and force of a bulldozer would do. *Jesu Kristi* would be different for the pregnant African mother depicted suckling a grown man in a painting hanging on the wall of the Jesuit house of formation in Arusha, Tanzania. Still, *Jesu Kristi* would mean a unique reality for the husband of Mama Mercy, whose fervent plea for grace in chapter 5 was mistaken for an inadvertent confession of marital infidelity. And the encounter, identity, and significance of *Jesu Kristi* will be unique for us.

Questions for Reflection and Group Discussion

1. When you look at your own religious and cultural background, what images would best express for you the identity and personality of Jesus Christ as presented in the New Testament?

2. List some of the titles of Jesus Christ that you have encoun-

tered in popular African Christianity. Why do you think African Christians find them appealing? Do they appeal to you?

3. If Jesus had asked you the question that he addressed to his disciples in Matthew 16, how would you have responded?

—⟡—

Christ Our Guest and Liberator

This brief rite is a liturgical adaptation inspired by Guest Christology. It inculturates the person and the message of Jesus Christ as the guest-liberator in the lives of African Christians. In this liturgy, Jesus Christ comes as an unpretentious guest, seeking time and space to dwell in the midst of the Africans, who welcome him into their lives, where he is initiated, accepted, and proclaimed the liberator. He shares "the joys and hopes, the grief and anguish of the people of our time, especially of those who are poor or afflicted in any way" (Vatican Council II, Gaudium et Spes, no. 1).

This rite takes place in the family of God, that is, the Christian community. Family of God is a preferred African metaphor for church. It evokes the memories of all the members of the family, including the living dead and the yet-unborn, who are "afflicted in any way" and in need of liberation. In addition, it celebrates Christ as the Word who takes flesh, dwells in our midst (John 1:14), and frees us from the shackles of sin, oppression, and injustice.

The Rite

All members of the community gather to welcome Christ. An appropriate song or chant is intoned. The presider welcomes everyone.

> *Presider:* We gather as one family to welcome Christ
> our guest. He comes to us as one who frees us
> from the bondage of sin, oppression, division,
> and injustice; the source of blessing, freedom,
> and fullness of life for our community. Christ our
> guest, we offer you kola-nut, a sign of friendship,

fellowship, and welcome from our family. Accept it, and make our community your home. Christ our guest, share our joys and our sorrows which we present before you.

Member: (Our response is: "Christ, rejoice with us!") Christ our guest, our sons and daughters are fruitful in birth and we are blessed with strong and faithful brothers and sisters.

All: Christ, rejoice with us!

Member: Christ our guest, our land is well watered and the yield of our harvest is bountiful.

All: Christ, rejoice with us!

Member: (Our response is: "Christ, free us!") Christ our liberator, our land is also plagued by sickness and diseases of all kinds: malaria, AIDS, meningitis . . .

All: Christ, free us!

Member: Christ our liberator, we are burdened by unemployment and unfair economic structural adjustment programs.

All: Christ, free us!

Member: Christ our liberator, we are oppressed by countless forms of injustice, we are saddled with the burden of corruption, and we do not love one another as we should.

All: Christ, free us!

Member: Christ our liberator, our hopes and aspirations are assailed by many setbacks, such as tribalism, ethnic hatred, division, and violence.

All: Christ, free us!

Presider: Christ our guest, our liberator, we offer you our joys and our sorrows; give rest and peace to our troubled hearts; may peace and justice reign in our community, and freedom be proclaimed to all of God's children.

All: We agree. Let it be so, Amen!

7

The Church Looked Like the Open Mouth of the Evil Forest

Chinua Achebe's *Things Fall Apart* is a fascinating literary account of the encounter between missionary Christianity and African traditional religious expressions and beliefs. In chapter 4 we saw the story of the preacher who had the unenviable task of explaining the Holy Trinity to an incredulous group of villagers. The story does not end there. The missionaries persevered. As time went on, despite the obvious differences between the two theologies, the missionaries began to make remarkable inroads into the hearts and minds of some villagers.

> "We have now built a church," said Mr. Kiaga, the inter-preter, who was now in charge of the infant congregation . . . "and we want you all to come in every seventh day to worship the true God."
>
> On the following Sunday, Nwoye passed and repassed the little red-earth and thatch building without summon-ing enough courage to enter. He heard the voice of singing and although it came from a handful of men it was loud and confident. Their church stood on a circular clearing that looked like the open mouth of the Evil Forest. Was it waiting to snap its teeth together? After passing and re-passing by the church, Nwoye returned home.

Mr. Kiaga failed woefully in his attempt to win Okonkwo over to the new faith. But much to the latter's chagrin the interpreter achieved a resounding victory by recruiting his eldest son, Nwoye, into the church that looked like the open mouth of the Evil Forest. Nwoye ventured closer and closer, and the church eventually snapped its teeth together. Nwoye was in: "One morning Okonkwo's cousin, Amikwu, was passing by the church on his way from the neighboring village, when he saw Nwoye among the Christians."

When we think of "church" what comes to mind? I have no recollection of what, if anything, the catechist taught me about the church in my catechumenate days. At one time in my journey of faith seeking love and hope I would have thought of church simply in terms of a *building*, where people gather to praise and worship God "every seventh day." In fact, that was the first idea Nwoye had of the meaning of the community called church. Today, in light of Vatican Council II's theology outlined in the document *Lumen Gentium* ("Dogmatic Constitution on the Church"), some Christians would say that *church is first and foremost a people*.

The word *church* appears only three times in the Gospels, all in Matthew (16:18; 18:17). It occurs more frequently in Acts, where it is used to refer to the community of Christians in Jerusalem (5:11), the mission communities (8:1; 14:23), the local assembly (9:31), and the church spread abroad (8:3).

If we bear in mind what was said in the previous chapter about the theology and Christology of the communities behind each of the four Gospels, we see that *church* as used in the Gospel of Matthew shows an attempt by the evangelist to connect the formal founding or institution of the church with the intention of Jesus Christ. We could say that some indications of the future church are discernible in the preaching of Jesus Christ. Jesus preached the kingdom of God as a sign of the establishment of God's definitive rule over the whole universe. The church that eventually emerged looks toward this kingdom as its representation here on earth, but it does not coincide with its meaning and reality.

Some theologians would also claim that Jesus' actions, such as the choice and instruction of the Twelve and the Last Supper, which he intended to become a memorial meal ("Do this in remembrance of me"), also point to the founding of the church. It is a debatable point.

However we formulate the argument linking the foundation of the church with the intention of Jesus Christ, it is important that we make a clear distinction between a *juridical* foundation and a *charismatic* foundation. They mean different things. The former implies that Jesus provided a blueprint of the church he wanted to found, while the latter means that the origin of the church owes to the inspiration of the life, teaching, and example of Jesus. To this second line of thought belongs the idea that the outpouring of the Holy Spirit at Pentecost empowered the community of the risen Christ for the mission of evangelization.

The theology of the church, or ecclesiology, also traces the church's origins back to the earliest experience of covenant between God and our ancestors in faith. The remote origin is to be found in the covenant that God made with Abraham (Gen 17) and the subsequent preparation in the election of Israel as the people of God. God summons a people and constitutes them as God's own with the promise, "I will walk among you, and will be your God, and you shall be my people" (Lev 26:12; Jer 11:4; Ezek 36:28). The idea and meaning of church embody and announce this unique relationship between *God and the people of God.*

The New Testament uses the Greek *ekklēsia* ("church") to translate the Old Testament Hebrew word *qahal*, that is, the people *assembled, congregated, and constituted* by God. *Ekklēsia* designates the people whom God has called out to God's self. In other words, it means *the people of God.* This is the preferred image or model of the church that we find in the teaching of Vatican Council II:

> All women and men are called to belong to the new people of God. The people therefore, whilst remaining one and unique, is to be spread throughout the whole world and to all ages in order that the design of God's will may be fulfilled: God made human nature one in the beginning and has decreed that all the children of God who were scattered should be finally be gathered together as one. (*Lumen Gentium* [LG], no. 13)

The people brought into being by God are redeemed by Jesus Christ in the power of the Holy Spirit (*LG*, no. 4). Thus the church owes its origin to the Trinity.

As the people of God, the church is also a *communion* (*koinōnia*). This implies the actual experience of an inclusive fellowship, participation, sharing, equality, hospitality, mutuality, solidarity, and so on. Primarily, it expresses our communion with God through Christ in the Spirit. Since, as the African proverb says, those who eat together do not eat one another, it refers, secondarily, to all those who are in communion with one another by virtue of their communion with God.

There is a variety of images of the church whose origin we can trace to the Bible. We find, for example, the idea of the church as the *sheepfold* (John 10); *God's own field*, which is cultivated under the inspiration of the Spirit (Mark 4:26-29); *God's household*, built on the apostolic foundation with Christ as its cornerstone (Eph 2:19-22). The New Testament also represents metaphorically the church as the Body of Christ (1 Cor 12:12-30), which implies an intimate life-giving relationship between the church and Christ, who feeds, cares for, and loves his body (John 6:56; 15:1-11). As the Body of Christ we live in solidarity with one another (1 Cor 12:26). Furthermore, the church according to the New Testament is *temple of the living God* sustained by the Spirit (2 Cor 6:16). The Spirit endows the church with graces, gifts, or charisms for growth, building up the church, and for the good and needs of the church in the world.

As mentioned above, however, *Lumen Gentium* prefers to call the church *the people of God*. As a people the church is a living body animated and sustained by God. It is also an inclusive community of faith that gathers all who have been baptized in Christ, who empowers us in the Spirit to proclaim the good news to the ends of the earth.

Although I said above that the church is not the edifice, there is a *structure* to the church. As a structure it is made up of diverse peoples, with clearly defined roles and responsibilities. Ordinarily, in the Catholic tradition, we talk of *laity* and *clergy, consecrated religious* and *priests*, as the basic groups of people who constitute the church. In addition, there are a set of laws and doctrines that regulate the life of its members. Beside this structural side of the church we have the spiritual dimension: the church is a community of praise and worship. It is noteworthy that this was the first thing that the young would-be convert, Nwoye, and many of the villagers discovered about the church in Mbanta, and it totally captivated their minds.

> Then the missionaries burst into song. It was one of those gay and rollicking tunes of evangelism which had the power of plucking at silent and dusty chords in the heart of an Ibo man. The interpreter explained each verse to the audience, some of whom now stood enthralled. It was a story of brothers who lived in darkness and in fear, ignorant of the love of God. It told of one sheep out on the hills, away from the gates of God and from the tender shepherd's care. . . .

Such is the power of the church as a community of praise and worship!

Vatican Council II adds another important dimension to our understanding of the church: the church is a *mystery*. When we see the word *mystery* we immediately think of something hidden and obscure. According to the Letter to the Ephesians, nothing could be further from the truth. Ephesians *understands* mystery as God's plan revealed in Christ (Eph 1:3-14). As a mystery, the church is a sacrament of Christ. "The Church, in Christ, is a sacrament—a sign and instrument, that is, of communion with God and of the unity of the entire human race" (LG, no. 1). My catechist taught me that a sacrament means "an outward or visible sign of an inward or invisible grace." What is the visible sign of the church? The people. And its grace? Communion with God and the unity of all peoples. Therefore, it will be correct to say that the church contains and communicates the grace it symbolizes, that of communion with God and one another.

You Africans, What Do You Say That the Church Is?

Catholic theologians speak of inculturation, by which they mean the process of expressing the fundamental truths of Christianity in the local faith-dialect of the people of God. In the preceding chapter we saw how African theologians go about the task of inculturation in relation to the personality and identity of Jesus Christ in Africa. The same process applies to the theology of the church. There is such a thing as an African understanding of the church (an African ecclesiology). The mystery of the church can and ought to be experienced and expressed using African models. African Christians have their own way of being the community called church.

In the previous chapter I said a lot about the Jesus question, "Who do you say that I am?" In 1994, a landmark gathering of bishops, church leaders, and theologians from all over Africa (the African Synod) met in Rome and posed a similar question with regard to the church: "Church of Africa, what must you now become so that your message may be relevant and credible?" In reply, the African Synod made "a fundamental option of the Church as family." According to the Synod, "family" should provide the framework of our understanding of the church. We think of the church and express its meaning in our lives as family.

In many parts of Africa, family is an important value and dimension of religious, socio-cultural, political, and economic life. Social systems in Africa pivot on the family. When Vatican Council II declares that the church is the *people of God* and a *communion*, we understand this to mean that within the context of the African Christian community, the church is *family*. Therefore, the corresponding and appropriate model of the local church in Africa is *Church as Family of God*.

This model of church is deeply rooted in the way many Africans understand themselves. To take one obvious example, an African can hardly define himself or herself without reference to his or her immediate and/or extended family. My favorite illustration of this typically African value comes from obituary announcements in newspapers. Each announcement begins by stating the name of the deceased and then goes on to describe this person by listing the names of all relatives and family members: He was the husband of . . . , the father of . . . , the grandfather of . . . , the son of . . . , the cousin of . . . , the uncle of . . . , son-in-law of . . . , step-brother of . . . , the nephew of. . . .

To situate, then, our understanding of the church at this level is to acknowledge, as did the African Synod, that, "the African family is a living cell from which models of the Church and experiences lived in Africa are found."

It was on account of the foregoing that the African Synod made "a fundamental option of the Church as family." What theological rationale or warrants can we find for this model of the Church as Family of God?

Recall the interesting encounter between Mr. Kiaga and Okonkwo on the issue of the Trinity. Mr. Kiaga used a familial image to represent God: father and son. Okonkwo objected because of the truncated nature of this analogy: How can you have a family of a father and son that does not include a mother? Actually, it is possible to speak of the "Trinitarian family" in a way that allows us to stress the distinctness, unity, and communion of the three persons of the Trinity. In chapter six, Charles Nyamiti talked about God being the Supreme Ancestor (see Eph 4:6) who communicates life to all. In the same way, he maintains that we can talk of Jesus Christ as the elder brother "of the multitude of God's children in whose veins—thanks to the mystery of the Incarnation and Redemption—circulates the same life-blood of Jesus Christ," and who are molded and initiated into the universal family of God by the sanctifying love and action of the Spirit. To say the church is a family of God means that it is modeled on the relationship that characterizes our Triune God as a communion of uniqueness, equality, and mutuality.

Christ invited us to love one another—all men, women, and children. This invitation finds resonance and concrete application in the African experience of community and family life, which promotes the values of hospitality, sharing, solidarity, welcoming, and so on. The Church as Family is founded on this African actualization of the love of God and love of neighbor. It is a church built on love, rather than on mere mud walls, as Nwoye may have thought at the time.

The eucharistic meal is the center of unity of the children of God. We are fed from the one table of the body and blood of Jesus Christ. The Church as Family has a profoundly eucharistic identity, not only because it is a sharing in the body and blood of Christ and in the life of the family but also because it constitutes the center around which the family gathers in order to evoke its ancestral memories—"Do this in remembrance of me."

What are some of the positive values of the African family? The concept of family in Africa contains values, ideals, images, and symbols that can be effectively utilized to express the model of the Church as Family. These values include the following: unity, solidarity, participation, and co-responsibility; family-based and family-centered education; the family as a place where life is welcomed, nourished, nurtured, and revered; sharing in common with the living and the living dead; understanding, fraternity, mutual aid, trust, reconciliation through rituals, non-gender-based respect for age, tradition and authority; hospitality. . . . When translated into the model of the Church as Family these positive values offer us the unique possibility of creating a dynamic, living, and vibrant community called church.

Let me, however, mention a caveat. We cannot romanticize in a naive way the meaning and experience of family in Africa. No one can deny that today the institution of the family is a discredited reality in certain contexts. The reasons are not far-fetched. Family has become the place of abuse, where women suffer subtle and explicit psychological, emotional, physical, and sexual abuse and violence. Children are not spared: parents and relatives abuse and mistreat them in a countless number of ways. In the time of the HIV/AIDS epidemic it is now a well-known fact that conjugal life places African women at a higher risk of HIV infection. In some situations the values of family life barely transcend the narrow confines of tribal, clan, and ethnic affiliation. Often, family is inward looking, built on blood ties and exclusive relationships. As we often say, blood (consanguinity) is thicker than water (of baptism). This negative attitude can be transformed if we understand Church as

Family to include all God's children who are born from above (John 3:1-21) and whose point of reference is the one God and creator of all (Eph 4:6), not the clan or tribe.

All this should suggest to us that when we say the church is like a family, we have in mind a different and special kind of family—the family of God, which strives to internalize the positive values and overcome the negative attributes associated with the ordinary experience of family.

To say that the church is the family of God commits us to the very important task of transforming the prevailing images and practices of our church in a way that embodies the positive values of family. Thus, there are practical implications. For example, when we say the Church as Family is a place of hospitality, the community should be understood in an inclusive manner. It is not enough for a person to be in a relationship deemed irregular or immoral for that person to be summarily ostracized from the church called family. What about the attitude and practice of treating lay people, in particular women, as second-class members of the church and inferior helpers of priests and bishops? That would be contrary to the spirit and ideal of the church called family. That one is an ordained minister in the church need not become a license to lord it over the nonordained members of the church called family.

How to Build the Church as Family

In African theology there is often a hiatus between theological models and pastoral applications. The model of Church as Family is not just a theological utopia. It has many pastoral applications and implications, some of which I will outline in this final section.

One of the central planks of this model is the African experience of hospitality and welcome. In the church called family *all are welcome*. There is a *home* and a *place* of belonging for everyone in the extended family of God, from which nobody is excluded.

The church called family promotes diversity among all its constituent parts. If within the family there is diversity and complementarity of roles and charisms of all members, the community will be transformed into communion in diversity. This means a community that values and promotes the gifts and talents of all. Each member has an important role to play which is not predicated merely on his or her status as ordained or nonordained. This leads us to consider a contentious but crucial dimension of Church as Family, namely, the issue of women in the church.

For a long time the church has paid lip service to the dignity and ministry of women in the church. At present, in some church traditions, it is taboo to question the reservation of ordination to male members of the church. In the minds of many people this represents an injustice that not only weakens the Body of Christ but also hinders the full realization of its evangelizing mission. There are good theological reasons for affirming this position, but this is not a book about the ordination or nonordination of women.

Women play (or ought to play) a central role in the Church as Family. How could God have a son without first having a wife as his mother? This was one of the main stumbling blocks to Okonkwo's faith. How can we talk about the church as a family without recognizing the pivotal role of women as mothers and leaders? The church called family is first and foremost *her family*.

One often hears, "In Africa the woman is at the heart of the family." Or the woman is "the backbone and the stability of the family." These have remained largely empty declarations. In reality, she suffers the most as the victim of various forms of injustice, abuse, and oppression within and outside the church. Notwithstanding, the African Synod makes a bold and radical statement: *"The quality of our Church as Family also depends on the quality of our women-folk, be they married or members of the institutes of the consecrated life."* This implies that the quality of the church would be seriously compromised if women are denied full and active participation in the life of the church called family. To accord women a full and active role would include, for example, involving women in decision making at all levels of *her* church called family, formation of women for leadership in all spheres of the church and society, and full participation in sacramental ministry.

The privileged place of translating this model of Church as Family into reality is the Small Christian Community (SCC). The

SCC is the church in the neighborhood, which helps to promote communion and co-responsibility, and gives every member a sense of belonging.

Church as Family also challenges us to redefine and reform the structures of ministry within the church, so that new forms of ministry can emerge and be developed with a view to promoting collective and common responsibility for the evangelizing mission of the church. These ministries would include the following: community leaders and elders, ministries of the Eucharist, the sick, the word; peace and reconciliation; promotion of life, rehabilitation of widows and widowers, and so on. Within this framework every member is given the opportunity to exercise his or her special gift or charism in the service of the Church as Family.

Integrating the diversity of the community or church called family into a holistic community requires dialogue and mutual listening. Nigerian theologian Elochukwu Uzukwu speaks of the "listening church." Dialogue is a family affair. Family life facilitates dialogue because it has the singular capacity to assemble and welcome members of various faiths under the same roof. Dialogue is a tool for integrating diversity and pluralism and achieving complementarity and mutuality within the Church as Family.

So, let us return to our question: What do you say that the church is? Nowadays, in response, many African theologians talk about the church as the family of God. Such rich imagery has great potential for transforming our experience of the community called church into a life-giving and nurturing family.

As the story unfolds in *Things Fall Apart*, Nwoye eventually renounced his family and joined cause with the nascent community of Mr. Kiaga.

> He went back to the church and told Mr. Kiaga that he had decided to go to Umuofia where the white missionary had set up a school to teach young Christians to read and write.
>
> Mr. Kiaga's joy was very great. "Blessed is he who forsakes his father and his mother for my sake," he intoned. "Those that hear my words are my father and my mother."

Nwoye did not fully understand. But he was happy to leave his father. He would return later to his mother and his brothers and sisters and convert them to the new faith.

For his father, Okonkwo, this was an agonizing twist of fate. As the story goes, already he could imagine "himself and his fathers crowding round their ancestral shrine waiting in vain for worship and sacrifice and finding nothing but ashes of bygone days, and his children the while praying to the white man's god."

But who could begrudge Nwoye the joy of finding a community that satisfied the deep yearnings of his soul for a family that would value him for who he was rather than castigate him for not growing up man enough to be like his father? In the church that looked like the open mouth of the Evil Forest this young African convert found a congenial assembly, a hospitable congregation of the people of God. Some of them were outcasts and considered untouchables. Others, like mothers of twins, were marginalized, oppressed, and despised by society. A few, like Chief Ugonna, "who had taken two titles," were highly placed in Umuofia. Nwoye threw in his lot with them.

As African Christians, we have "forsaken father and mother" in search of a place called Church as Family.

Questions for Reflection and Group Discussion

1. What is the word for *church* in your mother tongue? What is the literal meaning?

2. In your opinion how can the model of Church as Family enrich our way of being church in the world today?

3. If Vatican Council III were convoked today, what aspects of the church would you strive to reform? Why?

A Community Prayer for Healing

God of life, owner of our bodies, healer in the night,
There is malaria hiding in our children's bodies.
Response: God of life, heal us!
There is tuberculosis lurking in the lungs of our weak
    brothers and sisters.
Response: God of life, heal us!
There is HIV/AIDS festering in the blood of our strong
    men and women.
Response: God of life, heal us!
There is meningitis creeping in our children's spines.
Response: God of life, heal us!
There is leprosy eating away the flesh and bones of
    our poor brothers and sisters.
Response: God of life, heal us!

—☙—

God of life, owner of our bodies, healer in the night,
Remove the heat of sickness that torments our bodies.
Response: Fill us with the warmth of life!
Remove the diseases that deform our bodies.
Response: Fill us with the beauty of new life!
Remove the weight of infirmity which crushes our
    bodies.
Response: Fill us with the strength of life!

—☙—

God of life, owner of our bodies, healer in the night,
Response: Heal us!

(*Inspired by the title of Eric De Rosny's book,* Healers in the
Night.)

8

Mama Maria, Mother of Sorrows

Chinua Achebe tells the heart-rending story of Okonkwo's second wife, Ekwefi, on the night that her only daughter, Ezinma, suddenly fell sick:

> Ekwefi knelt beside the sick child, occasionally feeling with her palm the wet, burning forehead.
>
> Ezinma was an only child and the center of her mother's world. Very often it was Ezinma who decided what food her mother should prepare. . . .
>
> Ekwefi had suffered a good deal in her life. She had borne ten children and nine of them had died in infancy, usually before the age of three. As she buried one child after another her sorrow gave way to despair and then to grim resignation. The birth of her children, which should be a woman's crowning glory, became for Ekwefi mere physical agony devoid of promise. The naming ceremony after seven market weeks became an empty ritual.

The women of my home parish in Benin City have a mother's group called the Confraternity of Christian Mothers. Their patroness is Mary, Mother of Sorrows (Our Lady of Sorrows). I often wondered why they chose this title. As one of the Christian mothers explained to me, Mary knows what it takes to be a mother in Africa. She knows the pain of childbearing in dire poverty, the heavy hand of infant mortality hanging over the celebration of childbirth, the daily grind of raising a child almost entirely on her own, and the agony of losing an only child, even watching it die of hunger and starvation. An African woman knows more hardship, pain, and suffering than her Western counterpart. For the Christian mothers of my parish, Mary or Mama Maria, as they prefer to call her, could have been an African mother. Like Ekwefi, she was a mother of sorrows.

Mary is no stranger in the Christian faith. Devotion to Mary has caught on like a bushfire in the harmattan across the Catholic landscape in Africa. Countless Marian devotional groups exist in Catholic parishes, groups such as the Legion of Mary, the Confraternity of the Most Holy Rosary, the Block Rosary Society, and so on. Others have disappeared, such as the Blue Army Society, which was founded on the message of the Fatima apparitions (1917) to pray for the conversion of Russia. As a young convert, I prayed countless decades of the rosary, recited an assortment of Marian prayers, and rattled off endlessly the litanies of Mary to invoke her help in securing the conversion of the communist bloc. It was the height of the Cold War, and apparently I was in the thick of it!

Besides the largely lay devotional groups, there are hundreds of female and male religious institutes of consecrated life, whose foundation and apostolic mission rest on a strong devotion to Mary. On the face of it, the cult of Mary continues to flourish in the church in Africa. Tensions erupt every now and then between the more charismatic-inclined groups and the devotees of Mary on the contentious issue of Mary's role in the overall plan of salvation. Generally, all would agree that devotion to Mary, Mother of Sorrows, has come to stay in Africa. This is further confirmed by alleged Marian apparitions in different parts of the continent, such as Rwanda, Nigeria, and Kenya.

By virtue of her mention and place in the New Testament, Mary is known to all who profess faith in Jesus Christ. She is specifically mentioned by name nineteen times in the New Testament, not counting the instances where she is referred to as Jesus' mother. Between them, Luke and Matthew devote four long chapters to the infancy narratives in which Mary plays a very prominent role. Outside the Gospels, Luke tells us she was present in the upper room praying and waiting for the day of Pentecost (Acts 1:14) when Jesus will send the Advocate to the nascent community of the Way, as the church is often referred to in Acts. She was with the disciples when the Spirit was eventually poured out on all who were gathered in the upper room.

In many instances in the Gospels we see that she has a special relationship with her son, Jesus. John mentions two striking episodes in Cana (John 2:1-12) and on Calvary (John 19:25-27). Her unique role in the New Testament earned her the reverent title of *Mother of God*. She is *honored* and *venerated* as such in the Catholic tradition. The underlying theology would argue that her status, which elicits or founds such devotion, comes to her "by reason of the merits of her son." In other words, as the African proverb goes, the mother of a king drinks from her son's cup.

Vatican Council II treats the role of Mary in a document (*Lumen Gentium*) that expounds its central teaching on the doctrine and meaning of the church. This implies that it is theologically inappropriate to place Mary outside or over and above the church. Mary belongs to the church of Jesus Christ as a disciple and model of what it means to be a child of God, redeemed by Christ and sanctified by the Holy Spirit.

From Eve to Mary

Theologians tend to understand Mary's role against the background of the Genesis account of the Fall and some indirect "references" to her in the rest of the Old Testament. Genesis 3:15; Isaiah 7:14; and Micah 5:2-3 contain what Vatican Council II calls a "prophetic foreshadowing" of her role in the history of our salvation in Christ. On the basis of the biblical evidence, there are interesting parallels drawn between Eve and Mary: a serpent appeared to Eve, an angel to Mary; Eve disobeyed, Mary obeyed; Eve conceived mortals, Mary conceived the God of life. While Mary may have been predestined to be the mother of Jesus Christ, as the doctrine of the Immaculate Conception would have Catholics believe, this fact does not undermine the decisive significance of her assent and cooperation with God's plan of salvation. Mary was obedient, but she was not the passive, clueless, and frightened teenager depicted in many paintings of the Annunciation. We have reasons to affirm her active participation in God's plan of salvation through her faith and commitment. As one poet put it, "God waited" for Mary; and with God, the whole of creation heaved a deep sigh of relief at her simple yes.

As mentioned above, an essential aspect of the doctrine about the Blessed Virgin Mary is the belief that God specially prepared her for her role as mother of the redeemer. This preparation came in the form of her Immaculate Conception, a "unique holiness" that allowed her to be conceived without the burden of original sin. Besides, her participation in her son's work of redemption does not end with the Incarnation and nativity. Throughout Jesus' earthly ministry, from the Incarnation through Pentecost, Mary is ever present as a compassionate listener, faithful disciple, and active apostle.

The doctrine also teaches that by God's special favor Mary is the mother of us all in the order of grace, that is, in terms of how we stand before God's mercy and love. In light of the importance of the part she plays in Jesus' work for our redemption, she stands as the one who bears our prayers and petitions to Jesus the Christ. Even in heaven, as one of us, she continues to intercede for us. This is not the same as saying she is mediator. The role of Christ's unique mediation is neither challenged nor undermined by Mary's intercessory function. Whatever role she plays derives its importance, meaning, and efficacy from the role of Christ as our redeemer. Without this link, we would be rightly accused and guilty of subordinating Christ to Mary. Vatican Council II teaches that in relation to the work of Christ, Mary has a subordinate role: she points to Jesus Christ, our mediator and savior.

The doctrine of Mary also affirms her motherhood of the church. This motherhood is an example and a model to the church, which is called to bring forth children for God through Word and Sacrament. Her virginity is also an example to the church of how to be faithful, pure, and obedient to the will of God. She alone attained the fullness of this fidelity, purity, and obedience. Where she is now, the church strives to be one day.

Finally, the doctrine of Mary is careful to point out that her cult is a cult of veneration, invocation, and imitation, not of adoration or worship. Caution is needed in the practice and propagation of this cult. The two extremes to be avoided are "false exaggeration" and "too summary an attitude." As Vatican Council II counsels, "Let the faithful remember moreover that true devotion consists neither in sterile or transitory feeling, nor in an empty credulity, but proceeds from true faith, by which we are led to recognize the excellence of the Mother of God, and we are moved to a filial love toward our mother and to the imitation of her virtues" (*LG*, no. 67).

The theology of Mary (or Mariology) has evolved considerably in the last few decades. A significant part of this evolution derives from the development of feminist theologies. One of the cumulative effects is the gradual shift away from the image of Mary as the domesticated and docile servant of the church to Mary as the icon of the dignity of women and an inspiration for resisting oppressive societal, religious, and ecclesial structures and attitudes founded on a warped image of the Blessed Virgin Mary. In the rest of this chapter I will develop a reflection on the "Hail Mary" and offer some examples of how this radical shift warrants us to see Mary and women differently both in church and society.

Hail Mary, Full of Grace!

"Hail Mary, full of grace. . . ." Many Catholics have heard this prayer recited in an endless marathon of rosaries. Perhaps we have used it ourselves as we *said* the rosary. In my imagination, I am tempted to reconstruct the story of the "Hail Mary," that prayer with which many Christians, especially Catholics, have become quite familiar. Let us consider this imaginative reconstruction of the Annunciation.

> The angel of the Lord appears to Mary. "Hail Mary," he salutes. "The Lord is with you!" But unbeknownst to Gabriel, this Mary is not a docile, immaculate, and inno-

cent Galilean girl simply waiting to be carted off to her husband's house at a moment's notice. This Mary is an African, and she replies pointedly: "The Lord is with me? The Lord is with us? If the Lord is with us, why have all these terrible things befallen us, me and my people? Why all the famine, wars, diseases, poverty, refugees, bad governments . . . ? Please talk to me about that, or else keep your salutations to yourself."

By now one can imagine Gabriel's uneasiness. The story is not unfolding according to the script. But the archangel is eager to get to the point of his visit. So he continues: "Blessed are you among women!" Mary replies with a scornful snort . . . , "Blessed? What do you mean blessed? If indeed I am blessed among women, why have my sisters and I become cheap commodities, bartered and battered, oppressed and abused by society? Why do we toil and labor without respite to feed, clothe, and educate our children, children of runaway husbands, only to be cut down by death at forty-one, because the World Bank and socioeconomic conditions have decreed that forty-one is the average age of an African woman? Why, Mr. Angel? Or did you say you were an archangel? Answer me."

Gabriel is visibly confused but equally determined to deliver his message. "Blessed is the fruit of your womb, Jesus. . . ." "What fruit of the womb? Who asked you for a fruit of the womb, when one in every five African children will die before their fifth birthday, and millions of African children die every year of malaria and other preventable diseases?"

I leave it to the reader's imagination to work out the outcome of this apocryphal account of the Annunciation. Some readers might dismiss it as a flight of fancy or a figment of the author's wild imagination.

Christians are accustomed to celebrating the Annunciation as good news, because they believe that on a particular day, many centuries ago, the angel of God announced to Mary the good news that she would conceive and bear a child "by the power of the Holy Spirit." That was good news for the world, and Mary was the first to receive the news. In her lifetime Mary received many different kinds of news. As we have just seen, she was sitting in her house, when an angel appeared and announced the Incarnation. She was heavy with child when news came of a census in Bethlehem. She was still nursing her baby when news came that Herod was about to kill Jesus, and so she had to flee into exile. She was at a wedding in Cana when they announced that the guests had run out of wine. She was in the synagogue when old man Simeon announced that her son, Jesus, would be the source of division and cause her heartbreak. She was in her house when news came that her son had become mad because he was so busy preaching and healing that he had not even the time to eat. Then, one day, news came that her son had been arrested, and we know the rest of the story.

How did Mary react to the different kinds of news that she heard in her lifetime? The Bible tells us something about how she reacted, which it does not say about any other person. Mary treasured all these things in her heart; she pondered all these things in her heart (Luke 2:19, 51). As an African proverb says, the heart of a mother is deeper than a well. But she was not mute: she spoke, and she questioned God. Most important of all, she prayed. In other words, Mary knew how to pray. She had a deep heart, able to communicate with God about those things that she heard and experienced.

There was one last piece of good news. . . . Mary was sitting in her house, mourning the untimely death of her son, when news came that Jesus had risen from the dead, that Jesus was alive again. We may suppose that her reaction was the same: "Lord, may your will be done." And she treasured all these things in her heart.

In chapter 3 I made the point that God continues to speak to us in many different ways, many different events, and through many different people. Mary offers an example of how to discern the will of God in all these things. She models how to discern the voices we hear, by treasuring and pondering them first in our hearts. But, above all, she shows us that the most important thing is submitting to the will of God. In her case, it was not easy, but she did. Today,

God speaks to us, announces to us that we too are to conceive and bear Jesus, the redeemer of the world, and we are to announce him in words and deeds to the world.

Devotion to Mary in whatever form it takes is not designed to put devotees to sleep. On the contrary, it wakes us up (opens our eyes) to the reality that surrounds us, and allows every Christian to cry out with Mary, "How can this be?" (Luke 1:34). Devotion to Mary helps Christians realize that they carry in them a promise already fulfilled, that the word was made flesh and now dwells among us (John 1:14). It is a reminder of how God stoops to look kindly on the lowly, how God hears the cry of the poor and does great things for them, how God pulls down the mighty from their thrones, raises the oppressed, fills the hungry with good things, and sends the rich away empty (Luke 1:46-55). And Mary is at the driving seat of these divine exploits. The idea of Mary occupying the driving seat recalls another dimension of her relevance for our day and age.

Blessed Are You among Women

A few years ago, I received a card that bore the title "Women's Work." On the front cover of this card was a painting of the Last Supper scene. At a glance, one looks at it with a certain feeling of familiarity. But something is different. At the center of the table, where we normally would expect Jesus to be seated, there is a woman named Prisca, presiding at the Last Supper. Prisca is the woman at whose house the church met (1 Cor 16:19), and who probably also presided at the breaking of the bread. Prisca is surrounded by eleven other women: Dorothy Day, nonviolent activist for peace and social justice; Mary Luke Tobin, auditor at Vatican Council II, leader of renewal for women religious; Aung San Suu Kyi, Nobel Peace Prize laureate and leader of the pro-democracy movement in Burma; Mary of Nazareth, mother of Jesus Christ, who stood against the mob at the foot of the cross with a small group of women when all others fled; Thea Bowman, Franciscan sister, visionary speaker; Ita Ford, Maryknoll missionary in El Salvador, martyred by the military dictatorship; Ruth Fitzpatrick, coordinator of women's ordination conference, long-time activist for human rights and discipleship of equality; Catherine of Siena, fourteenth-century Dominican nun, mystic and tireless servant of the poor; Edith Stein, a mystic, Jewish convert who became a Carmelite nun, refused to flee the Holocaust, and was killed in a concentration camp; Rigoberta Menchu Tum, an indigenous woman of Guatemala, winner of the Nobel Peace Prize for her work in organizing the indigenous people of Guatemala to resist military violence and dictatorship; and Teresa of Avila, sixteenth-century Spanish Carmelite reformer, mystic, and great spiritual writer.

The card's designer, Mary Lynn Sheetz, celebrates the lives of these women in the different experiences and ministries they each had, such as "Motherhood, spending time in Nazi prisons, resisting military murder with their lives, living and striving in poverty, speaking truths to popes and [political] powers, mystical prayer, service to the dying, giving their all in jungles, deserts and mountains, writing poetry and songs, defending families and peace. . . ." Finally, she says, "Women have given their bodies to be broken and their blood to be spilt in every part of the world, responding to Jesus' call to 'Do this in memory of me.' It is fitting that they should preside at the Eucharistic table in the re-creation of that sacrament."

This design may not qualify as a masterpiece, but it attempts to convey a simple but poignant truth, namely, that the glory of God is woman and man fully alive. The women painted on the card evoke the memories of millions of other women who give their lives in service of God and the church in Africa and the world. The church or the world may not always celebrate the lives of these women, but in their simplicity and active faith they touch the lives of others; they change our world, the same way Mary of Nazareth changed the life of each and every Christian by living her vocation of motherhood and discipleship to the full.

In a concrete way we can say that Mary's life recalls these women in our lives and in our world, whose presence, like hers, draws us closer to Christ.

Blessed Is the Fruit of Your Womb

In a continuation of the prayer of the angel, Elizabeth goes on to bless the fruit of Mary's womb, Jesus (Luke 1:42).

Among some African people, it is commonly said that when a child is bad, he or she belongs to the mother. But when a child is good, he or she belongs to the father. Not so when the child turns out to be a king. Among the Edo (Benin) people of Nigeria, that child is first and foremost the property of the mother—her pride and joy. The woman who gave birth to the king is entitled to an honor reserved for special people. The king's mother is revered. In reality, it is not the mother as such who is revered; it is her womb. The womb that gave birth to the king is treated as a sacred object, an object of ritual deference and public devotion. In Benin, that womb is called *eko n'bie okhai*; this expression translates into the formal title attributed to the queen mother: "The womb that bore the person of dignity and importance."

In many parts of Africa where the institution of monarchy still exists, the title of queen mother has great significance. In some cases, she is the real power behind the throne. Nothing happens without her prior advice and consent. So strong is this institution that it would be true to say, in a positive sense, that behind every successful king is a powerful queen mother. As such, the queen mother commands a lot of respect. She enjoys special privileges unthinkable for the rest of the womenfolk and menfolk. She is revered and considered the shortest and surest cut to the king's ears.

It seems that we have elements of these African traditions in Catholic traditions. In fact, that is an understatement: we have a very strong and ancient tradition of honoring Mary as the queen mother. What we have in the canonical Gospels is not enough to give her the honor and glory we think she deserves as the mother of Christ the King. So the church has created traditions that accord special honor to Mary. Catholics celebrate her birthday and presentation; glorify her Immaculate Conception; acclaim her Assumption and coronation, even to the extent of arousing the contempt and condemnation of Pentecostal and charismatic Christians. In particular, the title "Mother of God" is a stumbling block for many non-Catholic Christians. Viewed from an African perspective, it is a title that gives cause for serious reflection.

From the perspective of our African tradition it would be quite fitting to accord Mary all the honor and the glory as the queen mother of God. After all, we say in our African cultures that "mother is supreme." One of Chinua Achebe's characters, Uchendu, makes a similar argument:

> "A man belongs to his fatherland and not to his motherland. And yet we say Nneka—'Mother is Supreme.' Why is that?" . . .
>
> "Why is it that when a woman dies she is taken home to be buried with her own kinsmen? She is not buried with her husband's kinsmen. Why is that?". . .
>
> "Then listen to me," he said and cleared his throat. "It's true that a child belongs to its father. But when a father beats his child, it seeks sympathy in its mother's hut. A man belongs to his fatherland when things are good and life is sweet. But when there is sorrow and bitterness he finds refuge in his motherland. Your mother is there to protect you. She is buried there. And that is why we say that mother is supreme."

When Mary gave birth to her son, she had no idea what he would turn out to be. She kept her thoughts in her bosom and wondered a lot about his future, his destiny. "What child is this?" She asked this question at the birth of her son (Luke 2:19), and again after finding him in the Temple (Luke 2:51). Her puzzle was not helped by the fact that Jesus turned out different from or other than what had been predicted. The angel said he would be a Messiah, seated on the throne of David, but Mary's son turned out to be a street preacher of no fixed abode. The angel said he would deliver his people from bondage; Mary's son so antagonized his own people that they sought every opportunity to lynch him. The angel said he would save his people from their sins, but Mary's son was condemned and hanged on a cross like a common criminal. Mary's son was draped in a purple garment, crowned with thorns, and he hung limp, unable to help himself or others. He was not a king. How then could anyone look at a man like this and say, "Blessed is the womb that bore you and the breast that nursed you" (Luke 11:27)?

When we look at Mary, what do we see? Do we see a queen draped in assorted royal gowns? That is what we see in holy cards and pictures. We might need to put aside all the titles we lavish upon her in our endless litanies. Mary is too down-to-earth, too faithful, too unsophisticated to be the mystical rose, tower of David, Star of the Sea, and so on. It is neither the nobility of her carpenter son nor the titles we invent on her behalf that make us celebrate her. Mary is just a Christian, but a Christian who believes that God's promise to us will be fulfilled here on earth and in the world to come.

Devotions to Mary are a celebration of the fulfillment of these promises in our world today. She is taken up to heaven not because she is a grand and royal queen mother, but because she is a Christian, a woman of faith. "Blessed is she who believed that there would be a fulfillment of what was spoken to her by the Lord" (Luke 1:45). "Blessed rather are those who hear the word of God and obey it!" (Luke 11:28). Mary heard, believed, and obeyed the word of God. Jesus is the Word of God. This Word saves Mary and crowns her with the glory and the honor befitting a queen mother, the same glory and honor that God promises us—if we dare to hear, believe, and obey the Word of God, as Mary did.

I began this chapter with one of the titles of Mary common among African Catholic women—Our Lady of Sorrows. The title refers to what is traditionally known as the seven sorrows of Mary, the mother of Jesus, the most painful of these being the experience of standing helplessly at the foot of the cross and watching her son die a shameful death. Nowadays, they do not teach the seven sorrows of Mary in catechism, as they did when I was a catechumen. Maybe it is no longer necessary. After all, we are surrounded by so many examples of Our Lady of Sorrows in Africa. Not just any kind of sorrows but sorrows that are associated with womanhood and motherhood. Who are these ladies of sorrow in our midst today?

I remember a popular song that we used to sing in my parish: "There is a man I love so much, there is a man I love . . . his name is Jesus." Not long ago, I heard an updated version of the song: "There is woman I love so much, there is a woman I love . . . her name is Mary."

Questions for Reflection and Group Discussion

1. "'We are honoring Mary today; we are honoring Mary never worshiping. . . .'" How would you explain the message of this song to a Pentecostal Christian who is convinced that Catholics prefer Mary to Jesus?

2. Compose a list of proverbs in your language that refer to motherhood. How might these be adapted to explain the status and role of Mary in the history of our salvation?

3. What do you perceive as the main difference between "venerating" Mary and "worshiping" her? How might the Marian devotions be reformed to better reflect this difference?

───── ᘐ ─────

Mama Maria, Mother of all Mothers
(A Marian Litany)

Mary, a mother in labor, is not ashamed of nudity; help us to overcome all forms of injustice and abuse of women.

Mary, when a father punishes a child it seeks refuge in its mother's hut; draw us closer to the mercy and compassion of your son, Jesus.

Mary, a child on its mother's back does not care if the journey is long; by your prayers carry all refugees to safety and peace as you carried the infant Jesus to safety in Egypt.

Mary, a child cannot pay for its mother's milk; by your prayers may we find constant nourishment for our faith in your son, Jesus.

Mary, a child does not laugh at the ugliness of its
mother; by your prayers may we treat all women
and men with respect and dignity.

Mary, a person who has not traveled thinks his or
her mother is the best cook; by your prayers may
we free our minds from all forms of tribalism,
discrimination, and ethnic violence.

Mary, if a calf sucks greedily, it tears away its mother's
udder; by your prayers help us to overcome greed
and selfishness.

Mary, the earth is the mother of all; by your prayers
help us to use the resources of the earth with
prudence and care.

Mary, the mother of a great person has no horns; by
the example of your life may we grow in humility
and selfless service to all women and men.

Mary, we are born from the womb of our mothers,
we are buried in the womb of the earth; by your
prayers may we know the joy of a peaceful death
and come to the eternal happiness of heaven
together with all our ancestors in faith.

Amen.

(*Inspired by African proverbs celebrating the joy and dignity
of motherhood.*)

⌐⊝⌐

Prayer for the Gift of a Child

*I have witnessed firsthand the angst of many a couple, and in particular
of women, faced with the prospect of childlessness, yet desiring to
have children of their own. Their prayers and supplications are often
expressed in images, symbols, and metaphors pregnant with meaning.
They resemble the prayer of Hannah (1 Sam 1:1-18).*

God of life, deep source of all life,
Unlock the sacred grove of life within me.
Remove from me the humiliation of childlessness.
Do not give my enemies cause to rejoice over me.

God of life, deep source of all life,
Plant a seed of life in the fertile depth of my womb.
Make the egg of life grow unharmed in the moist bed
of my womb.
Do not allow the fragile thread of life to break in my
womb.

God of life, deep source of all life,
May the sweet cry of life echo from deep within my
womb.
May I know the joyful pain of childbirth.
May my neighbors gather around me to sing a song
of new life.

God of life, deep source of all life,
May my bosom be a restful place for the fruit of my
womb.
May my breasts suckle the delicate fruit of my own
labor.
May my back know the joy of carrying the gentle
load of my womb.

God of life, deep source of all life,
Hear my plea for life.

Blessing of a New Baby

African peoples believe in life as the greatest of all gifts. A new member of the family or clan increases its life force, brings a promise of prosperity, and guarantees its ultimate survival.

> May your face be radiant like the rising sun.
> May your smile brighten the cloudy sky.
> May your cries always find a gentle response.
>
> May your first steps fall on firm ground.
> May your first sounds speak peace like the morning dew.
> May your first teeth be as white as Kilimanjaro's peak.
>
> May your ears be open to the bidding of your mother and father.
> May your hands perform good works for your family and clan.
> May your head bow low in respect before your elders.
>
> Amen!

9

Our Fathers and Mothers Who Art in Heaven

An iron gong sounded, setting up a wave of expectation in the crowd. Everyone looked in the direction of the *egwugwu* house. *Gome, gome, gome, gome* went the gong, and a powerful flute blew a high-pitched blast. Then came the voices of the *egwugwu*, guttural and awesome. . . .

The drum sounded again and the flute blew. The *egwugwu* house was now a pandemonium of quivering voices: *Aru oyim de de de dei!* filled the air as the spirits of the ancestors, just emerged from the earth, greeted themselves in their esoteric language. . . .

Aru oyim de de de dei! flew around the dark, closed hut like tongues of fire. The ancestral spirits of the clan were abroad. . . .

The land of the living was not far removed from the domain of the ancestors. There was coming and going between them, especially at festivals and also when an old man died, because an old man was very close to the ancestors. A man's life from birth to death was a series of transition rites which brought him nearer and nearer to his ancestors.

Chinua Achebe alludes here to an important element of the African religious experience, namely, the belief in the continued existence and the veneration of ancestors. But his eloquent account of this reality does not speak for all of Africa. Contrary to common assumption, not all Africans attach equal importance or reverence to the role of ancestors in their religious worldview. Even today many would dispute their relevance and argue that ancestor veneration is a dying remnant of Africa's pagan past. For those who believe in their existence, ancestors are not far removed from their ordinary and extraordinary existence: there is coming and going between the land of the living and the domain of the ancestors. Many African theologians pay serious attention to this aspect of Africa's religious experience. As we have seen already, it even forms the basis of some attempts to create an appropriate African Christology and ecclesiology.

In this chapter I want to explore more deeply, from the perspective of African Christian theology, how the practice of ancestor veneration relates to another fundamental Christian experience, expressed in the creed as the "communion of saints" and the "resurrection of the body."

As an African Christian, when I profess faith in the communion of saints and the resurrection of the dead, my creed finds deep resonance in my traditional beliefs and understanding of the meaning of life and death.

By way of introduction, it might help to situate this possible link or relationship in the context of the history of religion in Africa. Many African cultures south of the Sahara did not have a literary tradition. There were no pictures, paintings, or texts. By comparison, Islam, Judaism, and Christianity documented their religious history in sacred books, religious art, and a variety of literary forms. This is not to suggest that Africans were simply bereft of any means of preserving, recalling, and transmitting accounts of their past. Africans "documented" the memory of their religious experience in different creative ways, one of which was narratives, in particular, stories. In fact, besides many other consequences, the coming of Christianity meant a confrontation between two cultures: literacy vs. orality. In order to appreciate the Christian experience, Africans had to make an important transition from their oral tradition to a new literate tradition. Literacy would have appeared as something esoteric in many African cultures at the time of early Christian evangelization. It came at a rather high price, namely, the loss of an oral tradition that had sustained Africans for many centuries, long before the advent of Christianity in Africa.

We need to keep in mind, however, another very important fact: this encounter did not represent the meeting of two alien traditions of communication, as it might seem at first glance. It helps to remember that Christianity, Islam, and Judaism have their roots in orality. Each religious account was a collection of narratives carefully selected, collated, edited, and subsequently canonized, that is, made official as an authentic account of their collective religious experience. These religions share this trait with African religion.

The Judeo-Christian tradition contains many accounts of the lives of women and men who are believed to dwell in the presence of God. They are commonly referred to as saints. Christian religious worship dedicates a feast day to them—All Saints Day (November 1). In the Catholic tradition the feast day of the saints is a day of obligation; Christians are expected to participate in eucharistic celebrations honoring the memory of these models of Christian faith across the centuries. When Catholic Christians recite their creed, they declare their faith in the existence of the saints: "We believe in the communion of saints."

In the Bible we find some interesting references to this practice of honoring the saintly departed. One example is Sirach/Ecclesiasticus 44-50. This section praises the great ancestors and refers to them as the illustrious and famous men and women of Israel. Sirach 44-49 celebrates Israel's faith in their ancestors and offers a list of "godly men, whose righteous deeds have not been forgotten . . ." (44:10). In this list we find people such as Enoch, Noah, Abraham, Isaac, Jacob, Moses, Joshua, and Caleb. To be complete, we should include Sarah, Mariam, Deborah, Ruth, Hannah, and many other women. Sirach names each of them "of blessed memory" because they lived "godly lives." Another text from the Bible comes from Hebrews 11:4-39, which praises the exemplary faith of our ancestors in faith, calls them a "cloud of witnesses" (12:1), and gives a brief but fascinating account of what each one represents for our Christian faith. They are praised as models of true fidelity, authentic worship, and faithful discipleship.

To return to the African religious worldview, stories and narratives are important elements of this worldview. Without pictures or paintings, narrative accounts were created and transmitted from one generation to the next, telling of the lives, times, and deeds of our forefathers and foremothers. As a child, I grew up on a staple diet of storytelling. Typically, stories of our heroes and heroines were told by adult members of the family. The children listened intently, learning every detail of the stories and waiting for the day when it would be their turn to take up the mantle of telling family stories, collective myths, legends, and fables. For the most part, these narratives preserved the memories of our ancestors, with whom the entire family and the larger community remained in warm communion. Thus, when Catholic creed and doctrine declare our faith in the communion of saints and the resurrection of the dead, they cause it to resonate with a fundamental aspect of my African religious experience. I will explore this link a little further in the following paragraphs.

In many parts of Africa people conceive of life as a continuum. As Chinua Achebe puts it, a person's life from birth to death is a series of transition rites which brings him or her nearer and nearer to his or her ancestors. Cameroonian Jesuit theologian Engelbert Mveng once characterized life in Africa in a similar manner. According to Mveng, a person comes into existence as a "monad" (single, alone), then he or she graduates to the level of a "dyad" (typically exemplified in marriage); when the couple procreate, they become a "triad." In this way the life of the community is quantitatively and qualitatively rejuvenated. Within this vital continuum, the people maintain a strong belief in the ongoing life of the beloved departed: we say that the dead are not dead, they are still with us. We call them the "living dead"; they remain with us as guardian spirits, men and women who continue—beyond the limitations of death—to share in the life of the earthly family. Death does not deplete the life of the community. Instead, through the active presence of the living dead, the community grows qualitatively, because, as ancestors, they have only one duty: to protect the lives of their progeny. In many different ways we celebrate them. We rejoice in their presence.

An ancestor is not just any member of our family who has died.

As we saw in chapter 6, there are certain conditions a person must fulfill before he or she can be declared and celebrated as an ancestor. This process is somewhat akin to what is known as canonization in the Catholic tradition, whereby a departed person is officially proclaimed a saint. In other words, he or she is declared to be a model of Christian living.

In Africa, an ancestor is a blood relative of the living community; this relationship could be of common parentage or shared ancestry. The family or community recognizes and celebrates its own ancestors. Without an identifiable family or community to which they belong, the dead are merely unfamiliar spirits floating above human existence. In the religious worldview of some African communities such unfamiliar spirits can cause great harm to the community. The living community also recognizes an ancestor as a departed relative who resides in close proximity to the Supreme God. Transition to the world beyond allows an ancestor the privilege of dwelling in the presence of the Supreme God. The family or community has clear expectations of its ancestor's role. In the ordinary life of the community an ancestor plays the dual role of intercessor and protector. The former is possible because of the ancestor's proximity to the Supreme Being, while the latter is a function of the continuing ties that the ancestor enjoys with his or her surviving relatives. To be recognized and celebrated as an ancestor, one needs to have left a positive legacy; an ancestor models exemplary character and life-enhancing qualities, skills, or behavior for the living community. Such exemplary character facilitates the perpetuation of one's legacy in the family or community. Finally and most important, an ancestor is someone whose presence we can still feel and with whom we can still communicate because of our love for that person. At different times, especially during festivals and family ritual celebrations (birth, initiation, marriage, reconciliation, and so on), the living community pours libation and offers sacrifices to its ancestors to invoke their presence and acknowledge their membership in the communion of the living.

Warm Communion with the Ancestors

The strong belief in the perpetuity of life in Africa and the close-ness of the world of the living and the domain of the ancestors can be illustrated with an example from the island country of Mada-gascar.

Some Malagasy people have a very fascinating ceremony for the dead; it is known as the ritual of keeping the dead warm. After a few years, following the death of a relative, the entire family gath-ers together to open the tomb of the departed relative, rewraps, and reburies the corpse or whatever is left of it. The idea behind this practice is quite simple. The people believe that after a while the departed relative's resting place grows cold. So it becomes necessary to wake him or her up, rearrange the resting place and rewrap the corpse, so that the dead can keep warm. The ritual is accompanied by great feasting and rejoicing. This practice is not just an exten-sion of the respect for the dead for which many African cultures are known. It has to do with belief in life that transcends physical death and in the continued well-being of the living dead as part of the community of the living.

For many African peoples, life in the hereafter as an ancestor is not an easy matter. Oftentimes there is a trial, a test, or an ordeal that the departed person has to undergo in order to join the com-munity of ancestors. Such a trial could involve crossing a river or climbing a mountain. The other side of this belief is that living rela-tives of the departed can make a difference to the final outcome of this test. They have a role to play in whether the dead successfully cross the river or climb the mountain. We can assist them with our good wishes, or even give the dead money for the boatman or to pay off any obstacles he or she might encounter along the way. And if life in the land of the ancestors becomes too cold, we can help them keep warm by visiting their resting place, rewrapping their remains, honoring their memory, and celebrating our communion with them.

As Christians we have been taught also to assist the dead with our prayers. We have learned that life hereafter could also be quite trying. In fact, we commonly believe that it involves some form of judgment that will decide the ultimate fate of the dead (Matt 25). In general, Catholics perform this function of praying for the dead quite well: they pray for the souls in purgatory and all the faithful departed. Just as we do for the saints, we have also set aside a day to pray for All Souls—all "our brothers and sisters who have gone to their rest in the hope of rising again." Our prayers help our brothers and sisters because we believe, as many Africans do, that as we were connected in life, so we are in death and in our hope for new life. That is why the Malagasy continue to keep their dead warm and some people offer money to assist them on their ongoing journey.

Underneath all these practices, whether Christian or traditional African, lies an important expression of faith in the power of the resurrection. In other words, these practices embody our deep belief in the truth that death does not end it all; death does not have the final word on life. Thus, the bones that have grown cold and dead will warm up again; God will not allow the dead to stumble on the mountain. Nor will God allow their boat to capsize. It is equally true that this belief reminds us of the fact that God and we are united in caring for the dead, shepherding them beyond their fears and wants from death unto life. Perhaps even deeper lies the belief that Christianity and African religion share: that the care is mutual. We care for our departed ancestors by keeping them warm, clothed, and fed—with libations and ritual offerings. In return, our ancestors watch over us—with intercession and protection. The prayers that we offer for the living dead warm their resting place and give them a hand in their journey to eternal life. Their ongoing care for us keeps us united with them in one communion of the living and the dead, raised to life by the life-giving resurrection of Jesus Christ.

There is a common phenomenon of undermining the role of ancestors in today's African Christianity, particularly in Pentecostalism. Ancestors or the belief in their existence is considered by some as a demonic and pagan practice, which should have no place in the experience of born-again Christians. Thus, when we become Christians we are encouraged to forget about our ancestors. Unfortunately, by so doing we also forget that as Africans—just like any other race or people—we too have had men and women who have gone before us, men and women whose lives are worthy of emulation, men and women who continue to watch over us because they still love us and because they are with God. Some of them are our fathers and mothers; others may be uncles, aunts, brothers and sisters . . . who have gone ahead of us and taught us how to be good people by the example of their lives. Our Christian faith teaches us that they are with us still, because they are close to God through the power of the resurrection of Christ.

The Blessed Living Dead

In addition to what has been said so far, I would like now to suggest one simple way of reconciling the Christian belief in the communion of saints with the African belief in the living dead. Keeping in mind the criteria in both religious traditions, we might ask: "What did those saints, those men and women, do to deserve a place with God in eternal life?" If we listen to the reason provided in the book of Revelation, we see that these men and women we call saints are those who have gone through a great trial and have washed their robes in the blood of the Lamb (7:14); they have washed their robes in the blood of Jesus. Very often Pentecostal Christians declare that they are covered by the blood of Jesus. For these ancestral saints, to be covered by the blood of Jesus meant they had to give their lives entirely to Jesus in all circumstances of their daily living. It meant giving up one's life if need be for the sake of one's faith in Christ. Pentecostal Christians also declare quite readily that they have given their lives to Jesus Christ as personal Lord and savior (see Rom 10:9).

Several passages from the Bible give us an indication of what it means for a Christian to be covered by the blood of Jesus and to give his or her life to Jesus. One of my favorite texts in this regard is the Beatitudes in Matthew 5:3-12. We can paraphrase them in light of this conversation about ancestors and saints who have been covered by the blood of Jesus and have given their lives to God: If you are poor in spirit; if you treat others with respect and compassion; if you mourn because of the injustice done to your brothers and sisters, if you work tirelessly for justice, equality, and human dignity; if you reconcile divided people; if you work to promote the common good of all; if you are a man or woman of peace; if you refuse to give up your commitment to faith and justice even in the face of persecution, "rejoice and be glad, for your reward will be great in heaven!" Such a person is indeed covered by the blood of Jesus, and his or her life is totally dedicated to God.

The saints who are with God have given their lives completely to God. That is why we call the men and women whose lives we celebrate and whose memory we honor "saints." From an African religious perspective we celebrate and honor them as "ancestors." They were poor in spirit; they were gentle; they mourned for the injustice done to the poor and oppressed; they hungered for justice; they were merciful to those who had been rejected in society; they were pure in heart; they were peacemakers; they were persecuted for the sake of what is right. The lives of these saints and ancestors challenge us to become living saints, that is, men and women whose lives are an example for others to imitate. Paul used to call the members of the church "saints" (Rom 15:25, 26, 31). This is who we are called to be as Christians. We are called to be saints!

Henceforth, we are not expected to look at the paintings of the saints, with a halo above their heads, or the ancestral staffs of our foremothers and forefathers, and say, "I can't do what they did." As Christians we have all received the grace to become God's special friends; the journey begins here and now, a journey that our saints and ancestors have successfully completed. Their lives remind us that we too can be Christians with a difference, people whose lives others can see as exemplars of God's invitation to love, peace, justice, compassion, solidarity. . . .

In discussing the question of who is with God or not, some Christians refer to the 144,000 people mentioned in Revelation 7:4 and 14:3 as the approved number of saints. This represents a partial or biased reading of the text. Revelation talks about 144,000 people who have been sealed on their foreheads with the seal of Jesus Christ. But Revelation also describes "a great multitude (of people) that no one could count, from every nation, from all tribes and peoples and languages, standing before the throne and before the Lamb, robed in white, with palm branches in their hands. They cried out in a loud voice, saying, 'Salvation belongs to our God who is seated on the throne, and to the Lamb!'" (7:9-10). This great multitude of men and women are our fathers and mothers who are with God as saints and ancestors.

Talking about the communion of saints and the resurrection of the body affirms our Christian faith in a life that endures beyond death. The belief in the presence of our ancestors is a constant and concrete reminder of this communion and the gift of the resurrection of the body—thanks to the resurrection of Christ.

Questions for Reflection and Group Discussion

1. Can you think of people in your family who have gone before you? Are there some who were generous, loving, and kind, who did good works while on earth, whose memory continues in your heart, who died in peace with God, and whose names live on for many generations?

2. Can you recall some practices of ancestor veneration that you are familiar with? How can they be reconciled with the Christian celebration of the lives of saints?

3. Do you believe that ancestors continue to play important roles in the lives of the living? How do these roles relate to those which Christianity ascribes to saints?

In the Presence of Our Ancestors

Belief in ancestors is a common feature of many traditional African religious expressions. Some African and non-African theologians have sought to draw parallels between African reverence for ancestors and the cult of the saints in Christianity. Ancestors in Africa are present in the ordinary events of the people's lives. They are present in particular at special occasions and celebrations involving the whole community. This prayer invokes the presence of some contemporary African ancestors—

who are not normally celebrated in the cult of sainthood—at the beginning of a significant gathering.

> William Edward Burghardt Du Bois, champion of Pan-Africanism,
>
> *Response:* Present!
>
> Kwame Nkrumah, champion of the unity of all African nations,
>
> *Response:* Present!
>
> Marcus Moziah Garvey, champion of Africa for the Africans, those at home and those abroad,
>
> *Response:* Present!
>
> Amilcar Cabral, champion of the liberation of the African peasants,
>
> *Response:* Present!
>
> Patrice Lumumba, champion of the democratic freedom of the African peoples,
>
> *Response:* Present!
>
> Nnamdi Azikiwe, champion of African nationalism,
>
> *Response:* Present!
>
> Tiemoko Garan Kouyate, champion of the political, economic, and intellectual liberation of the African peoples,
>
> *Response:* Present!
>
> Steve Biko, champion of the freedom of the African mind,
>
> *Response:* Present!
>
> Albert Lithuli, champion of the freedom of oppressed Africans,
>
> *Response:* Present!
>
> Jomo Kenyatta, champion of the freedom of the African peoples from colonialism,
>
> *Response:* Present!
>
> Ken Saro-Wiwa, champion of the rights of the oppressed minority African peoples,
>
> *Response:* Present!

Felicite Niyitegeka, champion of the unity and peaceful coexistence of all ethnic peoples,

Response: Present!

Julius Nyerere, Promoter of Ujamaa and African family solidarity,

Response: Present!

—☙—

Invocation of African Saints and Ancestors[1]

King Afonso I Mvemba Nzinga—king and apostle of the Kongo,

Response: Present!

Anthony of Egypt—hermit and abbot,

Response: Present!

Athanasius of Alexandria—teacher of the faith,

Response: Present!

Augustine of Hippo—doctor of the church, North African bishop,

Response: Present!

Josephine Bakhita—religious and former slave,

Response: Present!

Anuarite Nengepeta—virgin and martyr of the Congo,

Response: Present!

Stephen Biko—political activist and martyr of South Africa,

Response: Present!

Ken Saro-Wiwa—environmental activist and martyr of Nigeria,

Response: Present!

---

1. See Frederick Quinn, *African Saints: Saints, Martyrs, and Holy People from the Continent of Africa* (New York: Crossroad, 2002).

Felicite Niyetegeka—woman of courage and martyr of Rwanda,

Response: Present!

Catherine of Alexandria—holy woman and martyr,

Response: Present!

John Chilembwe—pastor and revolutionary of Central Africa,

Response: Present!

Clement of Alexandria—father of the church,

Response: Present!

Samuel Ajayi Crowther—African bishop of the Niger Territories,

Response: Present!

Cyril of Alexandria—bishop and doctor of the church,

Response: Present!

Cyprian of Carthage—bishop and martyr,

Response: Present!

Olaudah Equiano—freed slave and author,

Response: Present!

William Wade Harris—prophet and evangelist of Liberia and Ivory Coast,

Response: Present!

Trevor Huddleston—bishop of Sophiatown,

Response: Present!

Simon Kimbangu—founder of the Kimbanguist Church,

Response: Present!

Matthew Lukwiya—Ugandan physician and victim of Ebola virus,

Response: Present!

Nkosi Johnson—child activist and victim of HIV/AIDS,

Response: Present!

Albert John Mvumi Lithuli—Zulu chief and Nobel Peace laureate,

Response: Present!

Janani Luwum—archbishop and martyr of Uganda,
Response: Present!
Bernard Mizeki—catechist and martyr,
Response: Present!
Monica—mother of St. Augustine,
Response: Present!
Alice Mulenga Lenshina—visionary and evangelist,
Response: Present!
Christiana Ma Nku—South African healer,
Response: Present!
Origen—North African teacher and church father,
Response: Present!
Nnamdi Azikiwe—African nationalist and president,
Response: Present!
Pachomius—founder of Coptic monasticism,
Response: Present!
Leopold Sedar Senghor—poet and president,
Response: Present!
Kwame Nkrumah—pan-Africanist and president,
Response: Present!
Mwalimu Julius Kamparage Nyerere—servant of God
    and president,
Response: Present!
Patrice Lumumba—Revolutionary leader and prime
    minister,
Response: Present!
Simon of Cyrene—co-bearer of the cross of Jesus,
Response: Present!
Simon Iwene Tansi—priest and monk,
Response: Present!
Tertullian—North African Christian teacher,
Response: Present!
Kimpa Vita Dona Beatriz—African Christian mother,
Response: Present!

Jomo Kenyatta—freedom fighter and president,
Response: Present!
Dedan Kimathi—Mau Mau leader and freedom fighter,
Response: Present!
The martyrs of Uganda,
Response: Present!
The martyrs of the Christian Fraternity, Buta, Burundi,
Response: Present!

10

If Two Hands Wash Each Other, Both Are Clean: The Meaning and Practice of Inculturation

Mr. Brown's successor was the Reverend James Smith, and he was a different kind of man. He condemned openly Mr. Brown's policy of compromise and accommodation. He saw things as black and white. And black was evil. He saw the world as a battlefield in which the children of light were locked in mortal conflict with the sons of darkness. He spoke in his sermons about sheep and goats and about wheat and tares. He believed in slaying the prophets of Baal....

There was a saying in Umuofia that as a man danced so the drums were beaten for him. Mr. Smith danced a furious step and so the drums went mad. The overzealous converts who had smarted under Mr. Brown's restraining hand now flourished in full favor. One of them was Enoch, the son of the snake-priest who was believed to have killed and eaten the sacred python. Enoch's devotion to the new faith had seemed so much greater than Mr. Brown's that the villagers called him the outsider who wept louder than the bereaved.... It was Enoch who touched off the great conflict between church and clan in Umuofia which had been gathering since Mr. Brown left.

It happened during the annual ceremony which was held in honor of the earth deity. At such times the ancestors of the clan who had been committed to Mother Earth at their death emerged again as *egwugwu* through tiny antholes.

One of the greatest crimes a man could commit was to unmask an *egwugwu* in public, or to say or do anything which might reduce its immortal prestige in the eyes of the uninitiated. And this was what Enoch did. . . . Enoch had killed an ancestral spirit, and Umuofia was thrown into confusion.

Chinua Achebe's Enoch manifested such religious zealotry as to shock even the missionaries and infuriate his own people in Umuofia. As he understood it, his African religious worldview and the new religion were mutually exclusive. For the latter to survive and become rooted in Umuofia, the former had to be uprooted and eliminated, even by acts of violence. Either the people of Umuofia embraced the new religion and abandoned their heathen gods, or, in the words of the missionaries, they would be "thrown into a fire that burned like palm-oil." Enoch's extremism admitted of no middle or common ground. Today, he would be identified as a fundamentalist Christian. Fortunately, only a small minority of Christians in Africa still behave in a manner similar to Enoch's.

There seems to be very little support for this extremist and exclusivist attitude toward other religions in the New Testament. My favorite story of Paul's missionary journeys is his encounter with the Athenians (Acts 17:16-34). Paul had no doubt about the fact that he was the bearer of the true religion, and his audience only had to listen and be converted. His attempt to correlate his God with their "Unknown God" ended in a laughable failure— the Athenians erupted in laughter (Acts 17:32). Yet Paul neither resorted to violence nor called fire and brimstone on the stubborn Athenians. In yet another section of the New Testament we read about how God so loved the world that God sent Jesus into the world (John 3:16). Earlier in the same Gospel of John we are told that the word that was with God from the beginning became flesh and made a home in our midst. In more technical language, theologians refer to this moment as the Incarnation: God became like us, as one of us (see also Phil 2:5-11). However we interpret this event, the idea behind it speaks of dialogue, interaction, compatibility, and mutuality. Whatever is designated as "flesh" is not adverse to what is revealed as "word," or "divine." Our God can and does pitch tent in the midst of our world. This fundamental category of Incarnation serves as a backdrop for understanding inculturation.

In African theology inculturation is a relatively new term; it has a variety of interpretations. One useful exercise might be to try to translate it into African languages. My assumption is that it does not exist in many African languages; one would have to create a new word or expression to translate its meaning. Swahili, for example, uses the word *utamadunisho* ("refinement, civilization") to translate "inculturation." I want to show in this chapter that, notwithstanding the lack of a corresponding terminology in the African religious vocabulary, the experience of inculturation embodies an important way of doing theology and practicing the Christian faith today. There are some theologians who would dismiss it as unhelpful because they claim that it focuses mainly on superficial aspects of the Christian faith. Perhaps the following description can help us to understand its meaning, necessity, and relevance in theology.

The talk about inculturation emerged in the context of missionary Christianity. As we notice in the story of Enoch above, the encounter between Christian traditions of faith and worship and African traditions of faith and worship was not always smooth. There were real and deep tensions that characterized this encounter. Some missionaries labored hard to eliminate all things African, in the manner of Enoch. Yet quite a few of them envisaged the possibility of a common ground between faith and culture. Today, many Africans who have embraced Christianity continue to explore various ways in which their African religious traditions enrich their newfound faith and vice versa.

Thus, the origin of inculturation goes back to the debate over the relationship between the Christian message and people's cultures. How should we understand the relationship between faith and culture? Several related terms attempt to capture the meaning and scope of this relationship. Let us consider a few examples.

One term that desceribes the relationship between faith and culture is *adaptation*. It involves a selective modification of Christian faith and worship using elements from African religion that are considered compatible with the Christian message. In this sense, one hopes that the new will not completely supplant the old. Another term that has been used is *accommodation*. It implies that while not entirely accepting the contents of other religious tenets, Christianity allows for or tolerates certain aspects of African religion. The Rev. James Smith disapproved of his predecessor's (Rev. Brown) approach of accommodation. On occasion, the term *indigenization* has been preferred. It refers both to allowing Africans to assume local responsibility for the affairs of the community called church and to giving the faith a local flavor and color. In this way, faith and worship would be recognized as indigenous rather than foreign. A final term is *contextualization*. It recognizes the need to take into account the situation-in-life of the local people in understanding the meaning and practice of Christianity. Nowadays, some theologians and experts in religion talk about *translation* as yet another way of understanding the relationship between African religion and Christianity.

We should keep in mind some important aspects arising from the above distinctions. In many instances, the relationship between indigenous culture and religion and Christianity seemed unbalanced: the latter claimed superiority over the former. This claim precluded any form of mutuality or commonality. In case of conflict, indigenous culture and religion were expected to yield ground to Christianity. In the understanding of some African Christians, this is still the case. Thus, the possibility that African religion could contribute something significant to the understanding and practice of Christianity or that African Christians would receive the new faith in ways that would be compatible with the African religious worldview appeared very remote and suspicious. At best, missionaries and their converts treated African religion as a mere preparation for the fuller revelation of Christian faith; at worst, they regarded it as a heathen, diabolical religion, destined to be suppressed by zealot foreign missionaries and African converts.

It is fortunate that things have changed significantly since the missionary era. To think of African religion as merely preparatory or simply diabolical is contrary to the notion and practice of inculturation. To understand the meaning and practice of inculturation I suggest that we begin by looking at the different aspects of the term. My point of departure is to consider inculturation as a multidimensional reality rather than a unidimensional one. As one African proverb says, a person can see the sun from many different places. The same is true of inculturation; we can look at it from various perspectives in order to create a fuller meaning, not only of the term itself but also of its practice.

Just like the Incarnation, inculturation is a relational term: it involves an encounter between two realities. Christians have no difficulty in professing—in the words of John the Evangelist—that the word became flesh. Word encounters flesh and makes of it its dwelling place. John further indicates the nature of this word: "the Word was with God and the Word was God" (1:1). If word represents the side of God from the beginning, flesh represents the side of creation and creatures. Thus, God embraces our human reality in a radical and final way. A crude way of saying this is that God has stepped into our shoes; God wears our shoes. As with any relationship in life this encounter could generate some tension; it is hardly ever devoid of tension. Word and flesh are not the same thing. Each party has something to contribute to the process of encounter: questions, challenges, acceptance, rejection, giving, and taking.

If we go back to the conversation between Mr. Brown and Chief Akunna, we see that it was fraught with tension: each party believed deeply in the truth of his faith and tried to convince the other of this truth. Although neither got to the point of attempting to destroy the objects of worship of the other—as Enoch eventually did—the possibility of resorting to violence is never far from the process of inculturation. Many communities in Africa and elsewhere first experienced Christianity (or Islam) as a consequence of violent conquest spearheaded by colonial Europe. Violence, however, is not intrinsic to the process of inculturation: both parties, gospel and culture, Christianity and African religion, word and flesh, can and should be open to a process of mutual listening, appreciation, and transformation. The result of this process bears the mark of a true inculturation.

Inculturation is a dynamic process: the encounter between word and flesh is not static. Word *becomes* flesh. The experience designated by the term "become" can be demanding. It requires much effort, because this process grows through commitment, pain, and sacrifice. Word loses a part of what it is as word so that it receives a part of what flesh offers; in return, flesh receives what word offers, while letting go of part of what it is as flesh. This relationship grows over time and in space; it is not a given or a permanent state. It needs to be the object of a constant effort, search, and renewal. The realities themselves (faith, gospel, religion, and culture) are not static or closed: they are dynamic and open to growth and change. When Christianity encountered African religion, the expectation on the part of some missionaries was that that one would supplant and eliminate the other. Word does not suppress flesh; it becomes flesh and dwells in our midst. Christian faith recognizes and embraces the truth of African religion, just as African religion receives and celebrates the truth of Christianity.

Inculturation is an integral process: it is not limited to only one facet of life; it covers all aspects of life. One of the reasons why some theologians have questioned the relevance of inculturation stems from the perception that it appears superficial. This critique is justified, especially when one considers the elements that have been labeled as authentic inculturation in Africa. For some people, inculturation has to do simply with using local African colors, songs, and musical instruments. One gets the impression that Africans have only song and dance to contribute to the message and practice of the Christian faith. Inculturation is not only about song and dance; as an ongoing quest for mutuality and comprehension between faith and culture, it touches and transforms the core of the symbols, gestures, words, actions, rituals, theology, government, and so on that make up Christian faith and African culture. In brief, the ultimate goal of inculturation emerges as an appropriate understanding and practice of Christianity. As Africans, how do we understand the gospel in order to live it according to our experience and situation in life? Pope Paul VI on a visit to

Uganda in 1969 made the insightful declaration that Africans have a right to have an African Christianity: "You [Africans] may, and must have an African Christianity." Inculturation designates the process of creating an authentically African Christianity, one that responds to our situation in life and makes a creative contribution to the meaning and truth of Christianity. In this sense, inculturation transcends our local situation; it has implications for how we understand and practice Christianity as a world religion.

Inculturation is a generative term; the realities involved in the encounter do not remain the same as the process of inculturation unfolds. Word became flesh; flesh too became word. Both are transformed. In this sense the process of inculturation is transformative. To speak of inculturation as generative or transformative goes against any imperialist attempt to impose Christianity on any other culture. As mentioned above, one of the underlying presuppositions of the encounter between Christianity and African religion was the idea that the former was superior to the latter. Missionaries presented the culture that underpinned Christianity as civilized and therefore superior. It had nothing to receive from the host culture and religion; it had everything to give to it, in order to save Africans from total damnation. This way of understanding the encounter between African religion and Christianity is outdated. The encounter involves tension but not violent conflict. If the gospel is the good news of peace, love, and justice, there can be no room for any attempt to suppress the culture of the people who open their lives to the Christian faith.

The attempt to destroy the religious beliefs and practices of Africans in the name of a superior religion demonstrates yet another illusion. Christian faith bears testimony to the belief that creation is the work of God. Several philosophers and theologians have affirmed the truth that nature expresses the presence of God in our world. This is true of all of creation, without exception. As a consequence, this understanding invites us to see God as preceding even the very attempt to preach the good news to the ends of the earth. My faith as an African is not an empty receptacle to be filled by a superior faith or religion; it is a dwelling place of the word who has become flesh and now lives among us. True Christianity recognizes, affirms, and celebrates this truth at all times. My faith as an African is not static; therefore, it will undergo change, in the same way that Christianity must undergo change when it takes flesh in Africa. Neither Enoch nor Rev. Smith could understand or accept this fact. They branded everything that they found in Umuofia as diabolical. They had the truth, a truth that had to be imposed at all cost. Yet when we look at the story of Umuofia we see rich religious and cultural beliefs and practices, such as the Week of Peace, reverence for the elders, veneration of ancestors, a profound sense of community, hospitality, and so on. Only a false understanding of the good news could have dismissed them as diabolical.

From the foregoing discussion we can identify some prerequisites of inculturation. Inculturation is a process; as such, we need to observe certain conditions if we are to reap the fruit of this process.

The most important condition is freedom. Inculturation cannot be imposed. The people who inculturate must discover for themselves the value embedded in the process. That is why the most authentic "inculturators" are the people of God themselves; inculturation is a not the fruit of theological speculation. Nor is it the sole preserve of theologians. Freedom also implies that the process of inculturation has to be the object of a free commitment to a relationship and an encounter. If it is not, then it becomes religious imperialism of the kind portrayed by Enoch and Rev. Smith. Theologians need to recognize and respect the innate sense of the faith of the people. This sense allows them to see possibilities of encounter between Christian faith and African religious and cultural traditions. Inculturation is not experienced as an intellectual possibility; rather, it is lived on a daily basis as a process of growth in the understanding of the Christian faith *as Africans*.

Another condition is mutual enrichment. We need to bear in mind that inculturation is a positive experience: it holds out to us some creative possibilities. We have a lot to gain from the process; we have a lot to receive from the process. The outcome enriches the gospel and culture; each must benefit from the process, even if it involves sacrificing something.

Dialogue is a critical condition of any authentic process of inculturation. There must be a free communication between the parties involved: Christian faith must listen to African religious sensibility. It is important that we pay attention to the forms of communication proper to each one, as we saw in chapter 9. Christianity, in the form that it has been preached in Africa, speaks in doctrines and dogmas; it speaks through experiences and events codified in sacred texts. African religion speaks mostly through what is directly perceived and concretely experienced: stories are told, myths constructed; histories are reenacted in song, rituals, and gestures; symbols and signs are created to express the truth of God's presence in nature. We have here different but complementary forms of communication. One of the mistakes of the early missionaries was to dismiss African cultural and religious outlook as preliterate and illiterate. They were reading the wrong texts; or, rather, they were reading African texts in light of their own texts. Learning to read the other's text is crucial to an authentic process of inculturation. This process is akin to learning a new language. The key word is *learning*. For this reason, narrative theology remains an important way of doing theology in Africa. It allows for dialogue and implies a sharing of views, values, and ideas; speaking with clarity and hearing with wisdom.

The process of inculturation must manifest a sincere desire to create something new. In other words, it has to be creative. The kind of creativity implied here has nothing to do with "slaying the prophets of Baal," killing the sacred python, or killing an ancestral spirit, as Enoch and Rev. Smith did in Umuofia. It is a creative fidelity to various traditions within Christianity and African religion. At the same time, this fidelity remains open to new ideas, approaches, and ways of understanding and living. This involves calling upon our imagination. There is no limit to how much we can create once we engage in the process of inculturation.

According to an African proverb, that fact that the sun turns all leaves in the forest brown does not prevent a farmer from recognizing the leaves of the great Iroko tree. Inculturation involves mutual respect, not arrogance. The attitude that underpins the process should not be one of superiority. The goal is not a leveling of difference but an affirmation of complementary truths present in each religious tradition's attempts to represent the face of God. Each must believe in the genuineness and richness of the other. Christianity has traditions, practices, and beliefs that span over two millennia. The same can be said of African religion: it has rich traditions, practices, and beliefs that predate Christianity and reveal signs of God's presence and action in the African religious universe. The process of inculturation ought to recognize the uniqueness and greatness of each religious tradition.

In addition to acknowledging the uniqueness and greatness of each religious tradition, we need to be careful not to gloss over the shortcomings, aberrations, and limitations. The practice of Christian faith or African religion in history and various contexts is anything but perfect. We have sufficient evidence from the history of both religions to demonstrate their failings and imperfections. In *Things Fall Apart*, Okonkwo's son, Nwoye, saw very clearly the limitations of his native religion and culture when he converted to Christianity. This young man's new faith provided answers for some questions that had been burning deep within his soul; neither his African faith nor his African culture could provide satisfying answers:

> But there was a young lad who had been captivated. His name was Nwoye, Okonkwo's first son. It was not the mad logic of the Trinity that captivated him. He did not understand it. It was the poetry of the new religion, something felt in the marrow. The hymn about brothers who sat in darkness and in fear seemed to answer a vague and persistent question that haunted his young soul—the question of the twins crying in the bush and the question of Ikemefuna who was killed. He felt a relief within as the hymn poured into his parched soul. The words of the hymn were like the drops of frozen rain melting on the dry palate of the panting earth. Nwoye's callow mind was greatly puzzled.

Yet the disruptive and disastrous consequences of the new faith for Umuofia and its culture and religion were clear for all to see. Okonkwo's friend, Obierika, expressed this in eloquent but heart-rending words: "The white man is very clever. He came quietly and peaceably with his religion. We were amused at his foolishness and allowed him to stay. Now he has won our brothers, and our clan can no longer act like one. He has put a knife on the things that held us together and we have fallen apart."

This suggests yet another virtue that should animate the process of inculturation, namely, humility. God's truth is bigger than any limited attempt at any time and at any place to express it. Each religious belief and practice approximates the truth of God's revelation. It is like the proverbial sun: it is bigger than the human eye can see. The failure to recognize this lies at the origin of great violence perpetrated in the name of God.

Humility leads to another important virtue: conversion. For true inculturation to take place there must be conversion of mind and attitude. Arrogance and claims to superiority obstruct genuine inculturation. There must be a willingness to let go of something and to embrace a new way of looking at reality and living out that reality. In his excellent book *The Anatomy of Inculturation*, Laurenti Magesa expresses the value of conversion so beautifully: "The missionary must be prepared to 'turn around,' to see things in a different light, that is, in a manner they have not seen them before. They have to confirm in the other persons their own identity even as they also learn from it" (Maryknoll, N.Y.: Orbis Books, 2004, p. 149). Both Enoch and Rev. Smith lacked this virtue of conversion. Their unbending determination resulted in a catastrophic clash that left both Christianity and African religion in a weakened position.

Another way of expressing the mutuality involved in the process of inculturation is to see it as an exchange of gifts and values. What both parties offer is of value: what each one is prepared to give must be valuable, not just peripheral or insignificant. The word became flesh; in the language of Paul, Christ "did not regard equality with God as something to be exploited" (Phil 2:6). It was something valuable that the word offered to the flesh; in return, the flesh made it possible for the word to dwell among us.

As mentioned above, inculturation is not simply the fruit of our theological speculation. It presupposes a deep encounter with the word who became flesh. Therefore, inculturation has to mirror the pattern of Christ's Incarnation as the true model of incultura-tion. "The Word became flesh and lived among us." The event of the Word living in our midst means good news for our world; it is a saving message. Therefore, the ultimate aim, goal, or objective of inculturation emerges as salvation. What is attained must lead to newness and fullness of life (John 10:10). The opposite would simply not be Christian.

Finally, inculturation is a charismatic experience; it is ani-mated by the Spirit of the risen Christ. The gifts that we exchange come from the Spirit. We cannot predetermine how these gifts will manifest themselves or what the outcome of the process will be. Inculturation is truly the work of the Creator-Spirit, which blows wherever she wills. It contains an element of surprise; the outcome can surprise us, something that we need to be prepared to recog-nize and embrace in faith.

When asked to describe the reality known as inculturation, the late superior general of the Society of Jesus (the Jesuits), Fr. Pedro Arrupe, had this to say:

> Inculturation is the Incarnation of Christian life and of the Christian message in a particular cultural context, in such a way that this experience not only finds expression through elements proper to the culture in question, but becomes a principle that animates, directs and unifies the culture, transforming and remaking it so as to bring about "new creation."

In a profound way, his words capture the meaning and prac-tice of inculturation. They show how central to Christian faith is this process that makes all things new, especially in the context of Africa.

Questions for Reflection and Group Discussion

1. Based on your reading of this chapter, how would you trans-late the term "inculturation" into your language and in what ways could it change your understanding of your Christian faith?

2. How was Christianity introduced into your culture? Was it a process of mutual respect and dialogue, or was it imposed by force and violence?

3. In what ways do your African religious beliefs and practices influence your Christian faith? Do you find tension between both or mutuality and complementarity?

⊖

A Farmer's Prayer (Before Planting)

The earth, for many African peoples, is like a mother, often revered as a goddess in its own right. Out if its abundant womb the earth produces plenty for the land and the people. It is usual for a farmer to invoke the spirit of great Mother Earth before planting in order to ask for plentiful rain, a bountiful harvest, and the protection of his or her crop from the vicissitude of Africa's sometimes inclement weather. As the psalmist sings: "The earth is the LORD's and all that is in it, the world, and those who live in it" (Ps 24:1).

> Womb of the earth, great mother of unlimited
>   abundance,
> Pray, receive the seeds you gave us.
> *Response:* May they find life-giving warmth in the
>   fullness of your womb, and protection from the
>   burning sun.
> Womb of the earth, great mother of unlimited
>   abundance,
> Pray, receive the seeds you gave us.
> *Response:* May they find life-giving springs of water in
>   the freshness of your womb, and protection from
>   the ravaging flood.
> Womb of the earth, great mother of unlimited
>   abundance,
> Pray, receive the seeds you gave us.

Response: May they find life-giving shade in the
coolness of your womb, and protection from the
ruinous drought.

Womb of the earth, great mother of unlimited
abundance,

Pray, receive the seeds you gave us.

Response: May they find life-giving solace in the
tenderness of your womb, and protection from the
marauding locusts and soldier ants.

Womb of the earth, great mother of unlimited
abundance,

Pray, receive the seeds you gave us.

Response: May they yield a bountiful harvest of grains
for your children.

11

On the Other Side of Heaven:
Spirituality Brewed in an African Pot

But at that very moment Chielo's voice rose again in her possessed chanting, and Ekwefi recoiled, because there was no humanity there. It was not the same Chielo who sat with her in the market and sometimes bought bean-cakes for Ezinma, whom she called her daughter. It was a different woman—the priestess of Agbala, the Oracle of the Hills and Caves. . . .

At last they took a turning and began to head for the caves. From then on, Chielo never ceased in her chanting. She greeted her god in a multitude of names—the owner of the future, the messenger of earth, the god who cut a man down when his life was sweetest to him. . . .

The moon was now up and she could see Chielo and Ezinma clearly. How a woman could carry a child of that size so easily and for so long was a miracle. But Ekwefi was not thinking about that. Chielo was not a woman that night. . . .

As soon as the priestess stepped into this ring of hills her voice was not only doubled in strength but was thrown back on all sides. It was indeed the shrine of a great god.

The Christian tradition combines many spiritualities. Several Christian writers are revered as spiritual giants. The church recognizes them as men and women who by their own quest of faith seeking understanding, love, and hope offered a path to God, a path that their followers continue to find accessible, enriching, and meaningful. Some of these paths have a name. We speak, for example, of Ignatian, Franciscan, and Benedictine spiritualities. Some are associated with particular locations, like Assisi, Medjugorje, and Fatima.

The term "spirituality" does not always feature in the description of African religion. Yet, there is such a thing as an African spirituality. The question whether or not African spirituality exists is a moot one. Like Chielo the priestess, Africans greet and worship God in possessed chanting, in a multitude of names and ways that one can distinguish and identify as uniquely African. How do we identify and recognize African spirituality? What are some of its distinctive characteristics? To explore these questions, we need to take into account what has been said in the preceding chapters. The following caveats will help situate what I understand here as African spirituality.

As it should be clear to the reader by now, Africa is a very large continent. It has a population of over seven hundred million people in fifty-three different countries. Each one of these countries has many different cultures, languages, and peoples. If we take these factors into consideration, we can appreciate the difficulty of talking about "Africa." Therefore, we should avoid the mistake of speaking about Africa as if we were simply speaking about one country. When it comes to Africa, diversity best characterizes its geographical, cultural, and religious maps.

This reflection on African spirituality proceeds from a Christian perspective; like most African Christians, I am a bearer of a double religious heritage—African and Christian. Here, we must also keep in mind one very important general characteristic of the African religious mentality. This characteristic is something that many writers have noticed about Africans, namely, that Africans are a very deeply religious people. The truth of this statement manifests itself in many ways. Anyone coming to Africa for the first time cannot but notice the strong and profound sense of the divine that pervades the ordinary lives of many Africans. Often this has been misrepresented as superstition and fatalism. The awareness of the divine is so strong that you can see, hear, feel, and touch it in the way people talk, behave, even worship, sing, and dance. In a nutshell, the African universe is charged with a palpable spiritual energy; this energy comes from faith in the existence of many spiritual realities: gods, goddesses, deities, ancestral spirits, and so on. African spirituality draws on the energy that comes from this awareness that the human being is not alone in the universe; the universe delineates a shared space between creatures and their creator.

What I refer to as an awareness of a divine presence in the African religious universe predates the advent of Christianity in Africa. African religion and culture consciously fostered and developed this awareness. In a certain sense, it is not correct to speak of African religion, because most African languages do not even have a word for "religion" as an organized system of beliefs to which a person could either pledge or withhold his or her assent. For most Africans, religion is a matter of practice; it happens in the ordinary events and experiences of daily life. To live is to be religious; to be religious is to greet God with many names in the multiple circumstances of one's life here and now. In African spirituality, the experience of God is more important than theology or a discourse about God.

The experience of God as the Supreme Being is a shared feature of many African cultures. This experience also offers a way of worshiping God that is very much alive in Africa today. But there is no uniform way of expressing this experience of God in worship. As we say in Africa, there are many ways of seeing the sun. Worship and celebration of faith in God varies from place to place, and among different peoples. This diversity forms another characteristic of African spirituality. It is not a systematized experience, to be replicated from one place to another; it unfolds with every echo of God's presence resounding in the hills and caves where we encounter the great God.

The foregoing discussion has some implications for how we understand Christianity in Africa. First, when we talk about African Christian spirituality, we need to understand that it is Christianity which is a "stranger" to Africa, not spirituality. The missionaries did not invent African spirituality. Long before they came,

Africans had already developed their various ways of expressing and celebrating their experience of God. These ways included priests and priestesses, prayers and forms of worship, shrines, sacred places, sacrifices, taboos, and respect for ancestors. I am convinced that we cannot describe Christian spirituality in Africa in isolation of these African ways of finding and encountering God in all things; Christian spirituality draws on elements of African religion. It draws from the rich resources of spiritual, cultural, and ethical values that are already present in African religion. As an African, when I name God, I do so in a multitude of names derived from the hills and caves of my religious experience. Without this background it is hard, if not impossible, to identify what, if anything, is unique to African spirituality.

While it is the case that Christianity came relatively late to Africa, it is also true that it has grown very rapidly since the coming of European missionaries. Africa constitutes one of the main centers of Christianity today. Millions of Africans have openly embraced the Christian faith, and many African Independent Churches have sprung up. Statistics show that close to twenty thousand Africans become Christians every day, prompting some writers to characterize the rate at which Christianity is growing in Africa as staggering and astronomical. Many church leaders have publicly recognized the importance of African Christianity. To recall the words of Pope Paul VI: "You [Africans] may, and must have an African Christianity." The same can be said of African spirituality. In the rest of this chapter, I will highlight some aspects of this spirituality. I do not intend this to be an exhaustive enumeration of what constitutes African spirituality; this reality is not only vast, but it is also continuing to unfold and develop. Any attempt to circumscribe it will be limited and partial.

As hinted above, African spirituality is a very practical kind of spirituality: experience is more important than theory. Religion in Africa takes place as a daily and public affair. In some other parts of the world, such as North America, it is a matter of constitutional provision to confine religion to the domestic and private realm. This is hardly the case in Africa, where a very powerful sense of the divine permeates the lives of Africans. African spirituality recognizes the presence of God even in the most basic events and experiences of everyday life. For Africans, God is a God who sees all, is present in all, and acts in all circumstances of life. When we eat in Africa, we believe that we eat with God; we offer part of what we eat as an offering to God and to the ancestors. At this moment, eating becomes a religious experience, not just a biological necessity. When a child is conceived and born, we believe that God plays a significant role in the act of conception and birth. The moment of birth becomes a moment of thanksgiving for the gift of life, which can only come from God. In *Things Fall Apart*, a farmer could hardly think of sowing a seed without first offering prayers and oblations to God, the owner of the earth. Planting and harvesting alike represent a moment of encounter with God, who is the source of all good gifts. As Africans, whatever we do, be it work, travel, or celebrations of marriage, success, human achievement, or even death, we always believe that God is part of it. God is not introduced into this ordinary or extraordinary experience as a stranger. God makes it possible; we encounter God in it. Thus, living is an experience of discovery; we discover God who is already present in the realities of our lives.

The crucial point here is the belief that one lives under the constant, complete, and compassionate eye of God. This kind of experience is celebrated in Psalm 139: "O LORD, you have searched me and known me. . . . You are acquainted with all my ways . . ." (vv. 1, 3). This is a psalm that many Africans would address to God with confident familiarity. This aspect of African spirituality has its roots in African religion, a religion that emphasizes the practical and active roles that the different spiritual beings and personalities play in the daily affairs of people. The gods are part of everyday life, with a specific domain and assigned responsibilities. For instance, in some places in Africa, there is a god of hunting, a goddess of fertility, a god of divination, a goddess of the earth (planting, cultivation, and harvesting), a god of thunder, a god of iron; different occupations, such as wood carving, metal working, sewing, and weaving also would have personal deities. This has implication for our understanding of God: it means that there is no aspect of the life of an African that is unknown or alien to the divine. God's knowledge of us is complete. To put it simply, African spirituality brings home the divine in a very concrete sense of the term "home." We live with the divine in our homes, our occupations, our joys, our sorrows, our play, and our work.

Perhaps the most significant aspect of African spirituality derives from the African understanding of life. Simply put, African spirituality is a spirituality of life; it is a celebration of life in all its dimensions. The notion of life forms the ethical and religious compass of the African religious experience. Life is the operative principle in African religion: the goal and aim of human existence is life in its fullness. All our religious celebrations in Africa center around life, that is, on how to protect life from harm, celebrate it as a gift, and strengthen or prolong it in the community. Yet, for one who is used to watching North American or European television news channels, there seems to be a great deal of destruction of life on the African continent on a daily basis. One sees and hears of wars, natural disasters, road accidents, killings, and so on all over the continent. To say that African spirituality is a celebration of the sacredness of life raises some serious questions: How can we reconcile this respect for life with the shocking atrocities perpetrated against innocent lives in many parts of Africa? Before attempting to answer this question, we need to keep the following point in mind.

Given the characteristically sensational press coverage of the political and socio-economic situation in Africa in foreign news media, it is often quite easy to forget that in the midst of such misfortune Africans have not lost their respect for the sacredness of life. In our prayer, worship, and devotion the cry of Africans rings out as a loud and searing cry for life. Many would still remember the Rwandan genocide of 1994, when some Hutu bandits massacred almost a million Tutsis and Hutus. While the media focused on the horrific murder of innocent people, little if any attention was given to the stories of many Africans who risked their lives to save the lives of their fellow Rwandans. One story illustrates this point.

There was a Hutu nun called Felicite Niyitegeka who was in charge of an orphanage of mostly Tutsi orphans. Her brother, who was a member of the killing squad, wrote a letter to inform her to run away, so that she would not be killed along with the orphans. Felicite refused to flee; she refused to abandon the orphans entrusted to her care. Their lives were too precious, and she preferred to die protecting them rather than abandon them. She died, while shielding the orphans from the bullets of the assassins.

This is a tragic tale but one that highlights the extent to which an African will go to protect life. It is important not to allow what Africans believe about the sacredness of life to be distorted by what the circumstances of life in Africa, such as war and violence, have caused. From the moment a child is conceived until birth, that child and the mother receive special care and attention in the community.

In chapter 9 much was said about the perpetuity of life in African religion. There is yet another fascinating aspect of this vitalistic conception. To recall what was treated in chapter 4, life is an expansive and inclusive reality. The African's respect for life also extends to and encompasses nature. Life is not the isolated quality of an individual existence; it is solidarity with nature (animal, plant, and geo-ecological life) and the rest of the universe. Nature guarantees the sustenance of the people (land, rain, and crops). Thus, Africans believe in a comprehensive connection among all the occupants of this universe. For this reason, many elements of the environment are protected and conserved as a matter of religious conviction. In Africa there are sacred forests that cannot be destroyed; there are sacred trees that may not be harmed; there are rivers, mountains, streams, hills, and animals whose existence is linked to the survival of the community. These may not be destroyed, because, in addition to being linked to the survival of the community, they are considered to be the abode or messengers of the gods, goddesses, deities, and ancestral spirits.

Many African societies believe that nature provides a cure for all kinds of ailments. In *Things Fall Apart*, when Okonkwo's young daughter, Ezinma, fell sick in the middle of the night, he immediately "took his machete and went into the bush to collect the leaves and grasses and barks of trees that went into making the medicine for *iba* (fever)." In cities and villages in Africa, the art of herbal medicine continues to thrive as an alternative or a complement to orthodox biomedical practice. When a cure is needed, many Africans turn to nature: herbs, seeds, leaves, shoots, barks, roots, and the like to find a cure for their ailments. This practice is founded on the religious belief that nature is sacred and contains healing properties. It is understandable that people who have this belief will be reluctant to adopt practices that destroy or harm their natural environment.

Africans also believe that nature is a privileged locus for encountering the gods, goddesses, deities, and ancestral spirits. Many independent churches hold special prayer and worship services on mountain tops, hills, caves, beaches, and clearings in the forest. Some African societies identify elements of nature as divinities. For example, to repeat some of the examples mentioned above, there is the goddess of the earth, the god of thunder and lightning, and the goddess of the ocean. This kind of belief stimulates respect for nature and care for the environment. Where this respect is lacking or violated, the community can impose sanctions on the offending party. One still finds some Africans who refuse to kill and eat certain animals, not because they are ritually unclean but because they are considered to be sacred. For instance, the Edo of Nigeria call the swallow "God's bird," and so it cannot be harmed.

In a world progressively endangered by deforestation, desertification, global warming, depletion of the ozone layer, dangerous carbon emission, greenhouse gas effect, and multiple forms of ecological degradation African spirituality emerges as a spirituality of stewardship, renewal, and affirmation of faith in the integrity of creation as gift and the shared patrimony of all humanity. African spirituality recognizes the vital connection between human life and the environment; it is a spirituality of balance, harmony, and wholeness, sustained by an active faith in creation as God's gift. When human beings violate or disrupt this harmony they open the way for natural disasters.

This expanded belief in the sacredness of life, along with the threat to life under various circumstances, has facilitated the emergence of a true spirituality of the cross and martyrdom in Africa. Africa has a number of saints, but there are also martyrs. In addition to Felicite, we have the Ugandan martyrs and Blessed Anuarite (of the Democratic Republic of Congo). In different ways, these African martyrs gave their lives for their faith, for the sake of new life on the continent of Africa. Yet again, we see another aspect of African spirituality: in standing for life, it stands against all forms of oppression and suppression of human dignity. In this sense we can represent African spirituality as a spirituality of justice, peace, and reconciliation.

Another important aspect of African spirituality comes from the emphasis on community and relationship. African spirituality is a community-based spirituality. In Africa, the individual is valued, but the idea of a strictly private or personal salvation is hard to sell to Africans. This has been characterized using several formulas, such as "I am, because we are"; "we are, therefore, I am." But the reality described here transcends mere formulaic niceties. The following story illustrates this point.

When European missionaries first came to Africa, one of them met an elderly African. The missionary tried to convert the African to Christianity. So, he said to the African, "You must give your life to Christ so that you can live in peace and happiness in heaven when you die." In reply, the African asked, "What about my ancestors, my forefathers and foremothers, would they be in heaven too?" The missionary replied, "Of course not, because they had not given their lives to Christ before they died. They will be on the other side of heaven, where there shall be weeping and gnashing of teeth." "In that case," replied the African, "I'd better remain as I am, so that when I die, I can be with my ancestors on the other side of heaven!"

The point of this story is that faith, salvation, redemption, belief, worship, life, and so on represent shared experiences for Africans. We can take another example—the idea of sin, which we considered in chapter 5. In Africa, sin or wrongdoing is not an individual and isolated act. An act is judged sinful to the extent that it harms the shared reality called life. Such acts have consequences for the entire community. We believe that a person's actions can pollute the entire community and disrupt the cosmic harmony. According to one African proverb, if one finger touches oil, it will soon stain all the other fingers. Conversely, forgiveness and reconciliation are not solitary affairs. Even after a person has made his or her peace with God, for example, through confession, it is still important to seek reconciliation with the community. Africans believe that God saves us as a people, not as isolated, disconnected, or disembodied individuals. In this sense, as we saw in chapter 7, the community of the church resembles an extended family rather than a nuclear family. As we also say, one person cannot both pray and say "Amen"; when one person prays, there must be others to respond "Amen." Jesus of Nazareth would affirm the same: "Where two or three are gathered in my name, I am there among them" (Matt 18:20). This is the kind of spirituality we practice in Africa.

In different ways I have alluded to worship, praise, and celebration as important elements of African spirituality. A few years ago, a documentary video was made to show the different aspects of liturgical life in Africa. That video was called "The Dancing Church." Africans love to celebrate and express their faith in song and dance. Body movements and participatory gestures contribute an important feature to liturgical praise and worship in Africa. When missionaries first came to Africa, many of them banned dancing, masquerade, drumming, and the use of traditional musical instruments in the church. African Christians were not allowed to sing, dance, or clap their hands in church. At most, they could only sing hymns composed in Europe with organ accompaniment. According to the missionaries, the ideal form of spirituality is an ascetic and austere practice. Therefore, any expressions of joy and celebration meant backsliding to the satanic ways of African religion and culture. This missionary understanding of worship represented a distortion not only of African spirituality but also of the meaning of praise and worship in Christianity. This negative attitude toward ritual expressiveness and exuberance in worship was quite widespread, but it was simply too alien to Africans. Since the inculturation of the liturgy began in the 1970s, Africans are now able to express their spirituality and faith in lively, spontaneous, and joyful song, dance, and rhythmic gestures.

In Africa, worship is never complete without singing and dancing; otherwise that worship would be considered cold and dead.

Every aspect of the liturgical celebration is accompanied by joyful vocal and bodily expressions. It is interesting to note that because of the effusiveness of Africans in matters of praise and worship, some people would claim that Africans are not able to pray or recollect interiorly and be in touch with the Spirit. Nothing could be further from the truth. The fact that Africans love to celebrate their faith does not mean that they are not able to contemplate that faith. A shared belief of many Africans is that anything that is good must necessarily overflow. As one African proverb says, a good pot of okra sauce cannot be confined to the cooking pot with a lid. It must bubble up and overflow. This means that what is seen on the outside manifests what lies in the depth of African spirituality.

Another striking aspect of religious praise, worship, and celebration in Africa is that even sorrow, failure, disappointment, and personal and communal misfortunes are celebrated in ritual songs, lamentations, or mourning songs. An African mother may be so overwhelmed by sorrow and burst into song, often in supplication to the God "who gives and takes." African spirituality is a holistic spirituality. It is a spirituality of resilience and courage in the face of the multiple miseries that assault Africans and their continent.

To sum up the foregoing, African spirituality is an expressive and lively spirituality. As our way to God, this spirituality is strongly rooted in the daily experiences of human life, which are experiences of life and death, joy and suffering, failure and redemption. We believe that it is in the ordinary experiences of our lives that we encounter God. In African spirituality, prayer and worship are transformed through song, dance, and rhythm into a profound and enriching encounter with the divine. African spirituality is a spirituality of the *Magnificat*; our spirituality is a joyful declaration and celebration of the great things that the Mighty One has done for us (Luke 1:49).

Questions for Reflection and Group Discussion

1. Identify two or three ways in which African Christian spirituality differs from Western Christian spirituality.

2. How would you describe African spirituality to someone who is coming to Africa for the first time?

3. How would you translate the word "spirituality" in your local language? What particular meaning or feature would it have in your local language?

—◯—

A Communal Gratitude to God for the Fruit of the Earth Grace before Meals

God of abundance,
You touch the grain of corn in the womb of the earth,
   Response: It yields a hundredfold of ears.
You touch the grain of rice in the swampy valleys,
   Response: It yields a hundredfold of ears.
You touch the grain of millet in the flat savannah,
Response: It yields a hundredfold of ears.

God of abundance,
Deliver us from the selfishness of eating alone,
   Response: For the person who eats alone dies alone.
Deliver us from the selfishness of hoarding the fruit of
   the earth,
   Response: For to eat too much leaves you with a
   swollen stomach.
Deliver us from the selfishness that causes enmity,
   Response: For those who eat together never eat one
   another.
Amen.

(Inspired by the three proverbs used in the responses of the second half of this prayer.)

—⟲—

To the God of Countless Gifts, Thanks!
Grace after Meals

God of countless gifts,
For the sorghum of yesterday,
Response: We give you thanks.
For the *fufu* of today,
Response: We give you thanks.
For the couscous of tomorrow,
Response: We give you thanks.

(Inspired by two African proverbs: "The one who gives thanks for the gift of yesterday will receive another gift tomorrow"; and "The person who says 'Thanks' makes him-/herself worthy of another gift.")

Postscript

Theology Brewed in an African Pot serves a dual purpose. It represents my attempt to reflect on some theological issues from an African perspective. By so doing this book also introduces readers to the discipline known as theology and its branches, such as ecclesiology, Christology, and Mariology. On several occasions, in the course of teaching theology and writing about Christian faith, I have often had to respond to questions on the relevance and necessity of *African* theology. Why not theology *pure and simple? Theology Brewed in an African Pot* constitutes neither an apology nor a justification of African theology. The days of finding justification for African theology are long gone. As I have shown in this book, theology is not a disembodied academic speculation on the nature of God, revelation, and faith. It touches on the profound quest for meaning and truth in a way that allows the believer to understand his or her faith in order to hope and love *more*.

Theology develops in context. Our encounter with God happens in time and space. Revelation, or God's self-communication, is immersed in history. Our deep and probing questions about the meaning of human existence arise from our experiences. Relating to God, self, and others happens within a concrete space and a defined time. Detached from our human experience and context, theology comprehends little if anything at all of who we really are or who we are called to be as disciples of Jesus Christ. The question one needs to ask of theology goes beyond whether it is traditional or if it conforms to the tried-and-tested ways of perceiving God and expressing the faith. The challenge facing theology lies in the extent and manner in which it speaks authentically and credibly to our experience today. We believe that God spoke definitively in Jesus

Christ, but we must continue to interpret, deepen, and appropriate for our day and age the meaning and implications of the word that became flesh and lived among us.

I firmly believe that theology does not float above culture and context. Doing theology is not an exercise in conceptual weight-lessness. It develops within the particular culture and context of the community that attempts to utter a word or two on the reality of God and the demands of faith for daily living. This word does not defy the law of gravity. My word on God echoes through the voices of my African culture and the multiple stories and narratives arising from experiences within my African context. It cannot be substituted for or suppressed by another voice from another culture and context. In reality, this implies that we cannot speak of a single theology wide enough to encompass the rich contents, expansive histories, and evolving traditions of faith across the globe. There are many theologies; African theology is one of them. In the midst of this diversity and pluralism, dialogue and mutual listening become essential virtues of any authentic theological enterprise.

Theology Brewed in an African Pot articulates some elements of African theology. This book does not deal with all the issues and questions raised in theology. I have not treated the sacraments, liturgy, ecumenism, or authority—at least not in any elaborate manner. My intention was not to be exhaustive; rather, this is an attempt to offer a quick sip, a very short introduction to readers and students of theology in Africa and elsewhere. *Theology Brewed in an African Pot* is not the final word on faith seeking understanding, hope, and love in an African context.

In terms of its context, Africa faces multiple religious, social, economic, and political crises. For people who believe in God, these crises provide an occasion for exploring the meaning of faith, hope, and love in the context of suffering. What is more impor-tant, these crises also become opportune moment to discover anew God's undiminished presence in the midst of our joys and hopes, trials and tribulations. The word became flesh and dwelt among us. This indwelling of the word constitutes a permanent and defini-tive act. The word has not abandoned us, and never will. Whatever disturbs our lives as God's people must find a place in our attempt to articulate the enduring communion between word and flesh in our particular context.

I have written *Theology Brewed in an African Pot* from the perspective of my faith as a Roman Catholic Christian. Much of the content of this book correlates some tenets of my faith to the context in which I find myself today as an African Christian. I hope that this process of exploring my faith as an African will stimulate a dialogue on the understanding of faith and its practice for Christians in other cultural contexts.

According to an African proverb, no one teaches God to a child. *Theology Brewed in an African Pot* offers a personal account of my experience of God as an African child. Knowing or encountering God is not a monopoly of religious and theological experts. As Africans, we know God from birth; we grow up in an environment filled with many experiences of God, and we live in communion with many spiritual beings and entities. We are never isolated from faith; we share a common space with God, the Supreme Being. Christianity teaches that God calls each one personally by name. Each Christian is called to articulate his or her faith journey in a way that speaks clearly and truly of his or her encounter with God's word. In reading this book, I hope that the reader has been stimulated to reflect a little deeper on his or her faith, whether or not he or she is an African.

Christian tradition often understands faith as a journey; some Christian writers speak of it as a race. The key idea here is that faith has a purpose and a goal. My hope is that *Theology Brewed in an African Pot* contributes in a small measure toward a clearer understanding of the goal and purpose of Christian faith and life in Africa and beyond.

⌐♉⌐

A Psalm of Praise

(Africa is blessed with an abundance of nature, all of which sings the goodness and praise of God. See Psalm 148.)

Radiance of the sun,
Response: Praise our God!
Splendor of the sunset,
Response: Praise our God!
Calmness of the moon,
Response: Praise our God!
Stillness of the night,
Response: Praise our God!
Brightness of the stars,
Response: Praise our God!

—⟋—

Rumblings of the thunder,
Response: Praise our God!
Flashes of the lightning,
Response: Praise our God!
Echos of the wind,
Response: Praise our God!
Freshness of the rain,
Response: Praise our God!

—⟋—

Softness of the grass,
Response: Praise our God!
Tallness of the trees,
Response: Praise our God!
Colors of the wild,
Response: Praise our God!
Music of the birds,
Response: Praise our God!

Dryness of the Sahara,
Response: Praise our God!
Immensity of the mountains,
Response: Praise our God!
Hardness of the rocks,
Response: Praise our God!
Coolness of the streams,
Response: Praise our God!

Children of Africa,
Response: Praise our God!
Sons of Africa,
Response: Praise our God!
Daughters of Africa,
Response: Praise our God!
Mothers of Africa,
Response: Praise our God!
Fathers of Africa,
Response: Praise our God!
Ancestors of Africa,
Response: Praise our God now and forever!

Suggested Readings
in African Theology

Achebe, Chinua. *Things Fall Apart*. New York: Anchor Books, 1994.

Bediako, Kwame. *Christianity in Africa: The Renewal of a Non-Western Religion*. Edinburgh: Edinburgh University Press, 1995; Maryknoll, N.Y.: Orbis Books, 1995.

Bujo, Bénézet, and Juvenal Ilunga Muya, eds. *African Theology: The Contribution of the Pioneers*. Vols. 1 and 2. Nairobi, Kenya: Paulines Publications, 2003, 2006.

Healey, Joseph, and Donald Sybertz. *Towards an African Narrative Theology*. Nairobi, Kenya: Paulines Publications Africa, 1996; Maryknoll, N.Y.: Orbis Books, 1996.

Katongole, Emmanuel, ed. *African Theology Today*. Scranton, Pa.: University of Scranton Press, 2002.

Magesa, Laurenti. *African Religion: The Moral Traditions of Abundant Life*. Maryknoll, N.Y.: Orbis Books, 1997.

————. *Anatomy of Inculturation: Transforming the Church in Africa*. Maryknoll, N.Y.: Orbis Books, 2004.

Martey, Emmanuel. *African Theology: Inculturation and Liberation*. Maryknoll, N.Y.: Orbis Books, 1993.

Muzorewa, Gwinyai. *The Origins and Development of African Theology*. Maryknoll, N.Y.: Orbis Books, 1985.

Index